Charles Hutchinson Gabriel

Special Songs

For Sunday schools, revival meetings, etc.

Charles Hutchinson Gabriel

Special Songs
For Sunday schools, revival meetings, etc.

ISBN/EAN: 9783337266080

Printed in Europe, USA, Canada, Australia, Japan

Cover: Foto ©Thomas Meinert / pixelio.de

More available books at **www.hansebooks.com**

Special Songs

By

Chas. H. Gabriel
57 WASHINGTON ST
CHICAGO.

For Sunday Schools Revival Meetings Etc.

ART VELLUM CLOTH.

Single Copy, postpaid, $0.20
Per Dozen, by Express, 1.75
Per Hundred, " 14.00
By Prepaid Express, 3c per copy extra

BOARD COVERS.

Single Copy, postpaid, $0.25
Per Dozen, by Express, 2.15
Per Hundred, " 17.00
By Prepaid Express, 5c per copy extra

FULL CLOTH COVERS.
Single Copy, postpaid, 25c.; per Doz., by Express, $2.50; per 100, by Express, $20.

PUBLISHED BY

Hackleman Music Co.,
712 Majestic Building, Indianapolis, Ind.

PREFATORY

SPECIAL

SONGS THAT ARE NEW.

"Sing unto Him a new song."

SONGS..

SONGS THAT ARE OLD.

"Sing . . . the songs of Zion."

Let all the people.. sing.

Chas. H. Gabriel.

SPECIAL SONGS.

No. 1. OVER IN THE GLORY-LAND.

C. H. G.   CHAS. H. GABRIEL.

1. We are on our way to a home on high, O-ver in the glo-ry-land;
2. We will join the song that the ransomed sing, O-ver in the glo-ry-land;
3. When the cares and tri-als of earth are past,—O-ver in the glo-ry-land;
4. With the lov'd ones gone to that shining shore, O-ver in the glo-ry-land;

There we'll meet and rest. in the by and by, O-ver in the glo-ry-land.
And for - ev - er praise our e - ter-nal King, O-ver in the glo ry-land.
Je - sus waits to crown us His own at last, O-ver in the glo ry-land.
We shall meet, oh, joy, meet to part no more, O-ver in the glo-ry-land.

CHORUS.

O-ver in the glo - ry - land! O-ver in the glo - ry-land! There with

all the blest we shall meet and rest, O - ver in the glo - ry - land.

No. 2. THE GREAT MEDIATOR.

C. H. G.   CHAS. H. GABRIEL.

1. There's a joy-ful mes-sage written in His word—Jesus is the great Medi-
2. On the cross He shèd His pre-cious blood for me, Jesus is the great Medi-
3. When before me all my years of sin a - rise, Jesus is the great Medi-
4. In His great compassion and His love di - vine, Jesus is the great Medi-
5. Earthly creeds may fail and kingdoms pass a - way, Jesus is the great Medi-
6. I will praise Him while my soul His call a - waits, Jesus is the great Medi-

a-tor! To the soul the sweetest mus-ic ev - er heard, Je-sus is the great
a-tor! From the grave arose with saving vic-tor - y, Je-sus is the great
a-tor! Un-to Him in faith my trembling spir-it flies, Je-sus is the great
a-tor! He be-held this fainting, dy-ing soul of mine, Je-sus is the great
a-tor! Countless worlds forever shall His word o-bey, Je-sus is the great
a-tor! I will shout His name while sweeping thro' the gates, Je-sus is the great

CHORUS.

Me-di-a-tor! I will praise Him, I will praise Him! He can
I will praise Him, hallelujah! I will bless His ho-ly name;

bind the broken-hearted, Jesus' love can make us whole; Halle-lu - - - jah!
Hal-lelujah! praise His name,

hal-le -lu - - - jah! He's the Lil-y of the Val-ley to my dy-ing soul.
He is ev-er-more the same;

No. 3. I KNOW THAT JESUS SAVES ME.

IDA M. BUDD.   Dr. S. B. JACKSON.

1. My heart is fill'd with joy to - day,   I know that Je-sus saves me;
2. When peace is shining in my soul,   I know that Je-sus saves me;
3. In calm or storm, in shine or shade,   I know that Je-sus saves me;
4. No oth - er joy can e - qual this,   I know that Je-sus saves me;
5. His blood doth for my sins a - tone,   I know that Je-sus saves me;

His presence brightens all my way,   I know that Je-sus saves me.
When sorrow's waves around me roll,   I know that Je-sus saves me.
In hope ful-filled or good de-layed,   I know that Je-sus saves me.
Since He is mine and I am His,   I know that Je-sus saves me.
His love re-ceives me as His own,   I know that Je-sus saves me.

CHORUS.

He saves me, He saves me, I know He saves me now;
He saves me now, He saves me now, I know He saves, He saves me now;

Oh, praise His name, His precious name, I know that Je-sus saves me!

No. 4. TELL THE STORY.

Rev. Neal A. McAulay.   Chas. H. Gabriel.

1. To the Christian legions comes the sweet command Tell the sto - ry,
2. There are countless millions in the gloom of night, Tell the sto - ry,
3. To the heathen nations o'er the wide, wide world, Tell the sto - ry,
4. Let us nev - er fal - ter in the work of love, Tell the sto - ry,

Tell the story,

tell the sto - ry, Spread the glo-rious tid - ings o - ver
tell the sto - ry, Shall the Christian na - tions give them
tell the sto - ry, Let the gos - pel ban - ner be - at
tell the sto - ry, 'Till the Mas - ter calls us to our

Tell the sto - ry,

sea and land, Tell the sto - - - ry o'er and o'er............
sav - ing light? Tell the sto - - - ry o'er and o'er............
once un-furled, Tell the sto - - - ry o'er and o'er............
rest a - bove, Tell the sto - - - ry o'er and o'er............

Tell the sto - ry, tell it o'er and o'er.

CHORUS.

Tell the sto - - - ry, let its mus - ic ring, Sweet-ly

Tell the sto - ry, let its hap - py mus - ic ring,

peal .... redeeming grace! .... Tell the sto - - ry, let the

Sweetly peal redeeming grace, redeeming grace! Tell the sto-ry, let the

Tell the Story.

ran - somed sing,'Till the world.... the truth em-brace...........
ransomed ev-er sing, Tell the sto - ry 'till the world the truth embrace.

No. 5. I'M SO GLAD THAT I LOVE JESUS.

J. E. H.   Arr. by J. E. HAZEN.

1. I'm so glad that I love Je - sus, For He is so dear to me;
2. I'm so glad that I love Je - sus, For I'm sure of one true Friend;
3. I'm so glad that I love Je - sus, For when comes the time to die,

I have found His love is sweet-er   Than all things of earth can be.
Thro' the shadows and the sunshine,   He will love me to the end.
He will bear me in His bos-om   Safe-ly to His home on high.

CHORUS.

I am so glad that Jesus I know; I am so glad, I do love Him so;

Rit.

I am so glad that Je-sus I know; I am so glad, I do love Him so.

No. 6.   JESUS, I COME TO THEE.

ADA BLENKHORN.   CHAS. H. GABRIEL.

1. Out of my darkness in - to Thy light, Je - sus, I come to Thee!
2. Out of my starv-ing in - to Thy wealth, Je - sus, I come to Thee!
3. Out of my sor-row in - to Thy peace, Je - sus, I come to Thee!

Out of my weakness in - to Thy might, Je - sus, I come to Thee!
Out of my sick-ness in - to Thy health, Je - sus, I come to Thee!
Knowing my joy will dai - ly in-crease, Je - sus, I come to Thee!

Thou who re - stor-est sight to the blind, Thou who art ev-er wondrously
All we can ask Thou freely dost give, Biddest the soul, in dy-ing, to
Out of my toil-ing in - to Thy rest, Here with Thy saints securely I'm

kind, Rest from my load of sorrow to find, Je-sus, I come to Thee.
live; Par-don and grace from Thee to receive, Je-sus, I come to Thee.
blest; With Thy great gift so rich-ly possessed, Je-sus, I come to Thee.

CHORUS.

Je - - - sus, I come to Thee, Je - - - sus, I come   to Thee!
Je-sus, I come, for Thou callest to-day; Thou wilt not turn a poor sinner away,

Jesus, I Come to Thee.

From Thy safe keeping to nev-er-more stray, Je-sus, I come to Thee!

I come to Thee,

No. 7.   MORE ABOUT JESUS.

BY PER. OF L. E. SWENEY, EXECUTRIX.

E. E. HEWITT.   JNO. R. SWENEY.

1. More a-bout Je-sus would I know, More of His grace to oth-ers show;
2. More a-bout Je-sus let me learn, More of His ho - ly will dis-cern;
3. More a-bout Je-sus; in His word, Holding communion with my Lord;
4. More a-bout Je-sus; on His throne, Riches in glo - ry all His own;

FINE.

More of His sav-ing ful-ness see, More of His love who died for me.
Spir - it of God, my Teacher be, Showing the things of Christ to me.
Hearing His voice in ev - 'ry line, Making each faithful say-ing mine.
More of His kingdom's sure increase, More of His coming, Prince of Peace.

D. S.—More of His sav-ing ful-ness see, More of His love who died for me.

REFRAIN.   D. S.

More, more a - bout Je - sus, More, more a - bout Je - sus;

No. 8.   LET YOUR LIGHT SHINE.

C. H. G.

CHAS. H. GABRIEL.

1. Let your light shine, let your light shine, That oth-ers may be-hold!
2. Let your light shine, let your light shine, And shed its beams abroad;
3. Let your light shine, let your light shine, That all the world may see

Its glow-ing rays perchance may bring Some wand'rer to the fold.
'Twill show the world you're not ashamed Of Christ, the Lamb of God.
Your works of mer-cy and of love, That they may fol-low thee.

CHORUS.

Let your light shine out 'mid the darkness on your journey, Let your light
brightly

shine, O let it shine;........ It may prove a beacon light to some
brightly shine;

trav'ler in the night, Let your light shine, brightly shine........
Let your light shine, let your light brightly shine.

No. 9. THERE'LL BE NO DARK VALLEY.

W. O. CUSHING.   IRA D. SANKEY.

1. There'll be no dark val - ley when Je - sus comes, There'll be no dark
2. There'll be no more sor-row when Je - sus comes, There'll be no more
3. There'll be no more weep-ing when Je - sus comes, There'll be no more
4. There'll be songs of greet-ing when Je - sus comes, There'll be songs of

val-ley when Je-sus comes; There'll be no dark val-ley when Je - sus comes
sor-row when Je-sus comes; But a glo-rious morrow when Je - sus comes
weeping when Je-sus comes; But a bless-ed reap-ing when Je - sus comes
greeting when Je-sus comes; And a joy - ful meeting when Je - sus comes

REFRAIN.

To gath - er His loved ones home. To gath - er His loved ones

home,   To gath - er His loved ones home;   There'll be
safe home,   safe home;

no dark val-ley when Je - sus comes To gath-er His loved ones home.

No. 10.   SUNBEAMS.

Rev. Isaac Naylor.   Chas. H. Gabriel.

1. Speak kind-ly to the err-ing one you meet up-on the way;
2. Speak gent-ly to the wand'ring one! O do not scold or frown;
3. Speak sweet-ly to the fal-len one, in ac-cents soft and low;

The bur-dened heart is yearn-ing for a word that you may say.
Re-mem-ber that his brow may some day wear a star-ry crown.
Tell of the pa-tient Sav-ior and His love, where're you go.

With anx-ious heart and smil-ing face tell of a Sav-ior's love,
Be pa-tient; soft in pa-thos speak; in earn-est try to win;
Re-mem-ber that when thou thy-self wert deep in sin and night;

And point the way that leads to ev-er-last-ing life a-bove.
A pre-cious jew-el, priceless gem, tho' stained with guilt and sin.
A ten-der word, a winning smile, brought com fort, joy and light.

Chorus. Faster.

Sunbeams, sunbeams, scatter them day by day; Sunbeams, sunbeams,
glad-ly, day by day;

Sunbeams.

scat-ter them all the way, Sunbeams, sunbeams scatter them while you
a-long the way, free-ly

may, Where'er you be, on land and sea, Scatter them all the way.
while you may,

No. 11.   **JESUS PAID IT ALL.**

Mrs. E. M. Hall.   John T. Grape.

1. I hear the Sav-ior say, "Thy strength in-deed is small; Child of
2. Lord, now in-deed I find Thy pow'r and Thine a-lone, Can
3. For noth-ing good have I Where - by my grace to claim— I'll
4. And when be-fore the throne I stand in Him complete, I'll

CHORUS.

weakness, watch and pray, Find in me thine all in all." Je-sus paid tt
change the lep - er's spots, And melt the heart of stone.
wash my garments in The blood of Calvary's Lamb.
lay my tro-phies down, All down at Je - sus' feet.

all, All to Him I owe; Sin had left a crimson stain, He wash'd it white as snow;

No. 12.   WALKING IN THE HIGHWAY.

E. R. LATTA.   CHAS. K. LANGLEY.

1. Are you walking in the highway Where the faithful all have trod?
2. Are you walking in the highway That will nev-er you mis-lead?
3. Are you walking in the highway, Or in ways of sin and woe?
4. Are you walking in the highway, Dai - ly, hour-ly near-er home?

In the road to life e - ter-nal, In the high-way of our God?
Where the christ-ian pil-grims journey, Who their Lord's commandments heed?
Do you seek the heav'nly kingdom, Or in. ways of pleasures go?
Then pur - sue the Ca-naan jour-ney 'Till the resting time shall come.

CHORUS.

Are you walking....... in the high-way!........ Are you
Are you walking in the highway, Are you walking in the highway, Are you

Are you walking......
walking in the highway, in the King's highway? Are you walk-ing in the highway,

in the highway......
Are you walking in the highway, Are you walking in the highway of the King?

No. 13. THE BEACON OF LIGHT.

REV. NEAL A. McAULAY.   CHAS. H. GABRIEL.

1. I was out on life's o - cean where tempests were wild, And the
2. When the deep un-der cur-rent my pro-gress would stay, And the
3. I will sail 'till the voy - age of life shall be o'er; My as -

bil-lows my soul did af - fright, But I lift - ed my eyes to the
wild tempests roar in their might, I de-pend on the beams that il -
sur - ance no . e - vil can blight, For I'll al-ways re - ly on the

head-lands of grace, And be-hold the bright beacon, the beacon of light.
lu-mine my way, I am led by the beacon, the beacon of light.
rays of my God, Shining forth from the beacon, the beacon of light.

bil - low - y sea, Till I reach the safe har-bor, the har-bor of rest.

CHORUS.

Shine forth in Thy beau-ty, O bea-con of light, Lead me on to the

D. S.

shores of the blest,........ Guide my bark as it sails o'er the
of the blest, .

No. 14. THE WORK OF LOVE.

C. H. G.

CHAS. H. GABRIEL.

1. There are those we must en-cour - age, Who are struggling and
2. Is thy broth - er faint and wea - ry? Go and help him his
3. Here a lov - ing word of com-fort; There an ac - tion of

try -ing to win; For we know not their temp-ta-tions, Nor the
bur-den to bear! Has he wander'd from the path-way? Go and
mer - cy and love; Scat-ter sunshine all a-round you, And the

CHORUS.

fight they are waging with sin. ⎰ Scat-ter deeds.... of kindness and love,..
lead Him to Je-sus in prayer! ⎱
Lord will re-ward you above. ⎰ Scatter deeds of kindness, Scatter deeds of love

It will bright - en the pathway a-bove...... Scatter deeds.... of
It will light the path - way to your home, Scatter loving words

love a-long the way That leads to ev - er-last-ing day........
all along the way That leads to ev-er-last-ing, ev-er-last-ing day.

No. 15. FOLLOW ME.

Mrs. J. V. C.   Mrs. J. V. Coombs.

Earnestly.

1. Have you heard the in - vi - ta - tion Which the Lord ex-tends to thee?
2. Now the call to you is giv - en, From your sins would you be free?
3. Still the gos - pel call is sounding, Will you heed the ear-nest plea?

It has sounded down the a - ges, "Leave the world and fol-low me."
Hear the Sav - ior gen-tly pleading, "Leave the world and fol-low me."
Je - sus calls you gen-tly, sweet-ly, "Leave the world and fol-low me."

CHORUS.

"Fol-low me,   fol - low me,   I will lead thee all the
"Fol - low me,   fol-low me,   I will lead   thee,

way."   We will fol - low,
lead   thee all   the   way."   We will fol - low,

we   will fol - low,   To the realms of   end - less day.
we   will fol - low,

No. 16. LEAD AND KEEP ME.

Copyright, 1900, by W. E. M. Hackleman.

HARRIET E. JONES. H. A. HENRY.

1. Lov-ing Sav-ior, lead Thou me,.......... Lest I wan-der far from
2. Oh, Thou ref-uge of my soul,......... Hold me in di-vine con-
3. Sav-ior, keep me day by day,......... All a-long my pil-grim

Lov - - ing Savior, lead Thou me; Lest I

Thee............. I am safe when in Thy care,..........
trol;............. What-so-ev-er may be-tide,..........
way;............. When my earth-ly work is done,........

wan-der far from Thee, I am safe when in Thy care,

CHORUS.

Thou wilt keep from ev-'ry snare. ⎫ Lead me,
Lead and keep me by Thy side. ⎬ Lead me, O my Sav - ior,
Lead me home, O bless-ed One. ⎭

lead me, Sav-ior, lead me all the way,..... This my

nev-er let me stray. lead me, This

constant pray'r shall be,.......... Sav-ior, lead me home to Thee.

my constant pray'r shall be,

No. 17. ALL THE WAY.

CHARLOTTE G. HOMER.   DR. L. O. EMERSON.

1. All the way my Savior leadeth me; Shepherd, Friend and Guide is He;
2. All the way my Savior leadeth me,   Nev - er can I doubt-ful be,
3. All the way my Savior leadeth me,   And communion sweet have we;
4. All the way my Savior leadeth me,   And, throughout e-ter-ni - ty,

And tho' clouds of darkness o'er me roll, There is joy and sunlight in my soul.
For He sweetly whispers in my ear, "Child, be patient, I, thy Lord, am near!"
Grace He gives me, and such peace affords, That I feel and know I'm all the Lord's.
I will praise Him for the love and pow'r That sustains and saves me ev'ry hour.

CHORUS.

Where He leads . . . . . . me I will fol - low, I will
Where He leads

fol - - low all the way . . . . Where He
I will fol - low, I will fol - low all the way;

leads . . . . me, I will fol - low, I will fol-low all the way.
Where He leads

COPYRIGHT, 1894, BY CHAS. H. GABRIEL.

No. 18. YOU MAY, IF YOU WILL.

C. H. G.   CHAS. H. GABRIEL.

1. If you will, you may know the glad-ness of your sins for-giv'n,
2. If you will, you may close the door and let Him knock in vain,
3. If you will, there are souls that you may lead to life and love,
4. If you will, you may sing in heav'n for-ev-er with the blest,

If you will, .. if you will, ... If you will, you may make the
If you will, .. if you will, ... If you will:—but His Spir-it
If you will, .. if you will, ... If you will, there's a crown that
If you will, .. if you will, ... If you will, you may meet the

If you will,   *if you will,*

an-gels sing for joy in heav'n, If you will, ... if you will.
may not ev-er strive a-gain, If you will, ... if you will:
you may wear in heav'n a-bove, If you will, ... if you will.
loved ones in that home of rest, If you will, ... if you will.

If you will,

CHORUS.

If you will, ... oh, hal-le-lu-jah, praise the Lord, I am hap-py in the

If you will,

prom-ise of His word;   Brother, you may share the blessing here and

hal-le-lu-jah!

You May, if You Will.

glo-ry o-ver there, If you will,......... if you will.......
If you will, if you will, if you will.

No. 19. JESUS, THE LIGHT OF THE WORLD.

J. V. C.   Arranged.

1. All   ye saints of light proclaim, Je-sus, the Light of the   world;
2. Hear the Sav-ior's ear-nest call, Je-sus, the Light of the   world;
3. Why not seek Him then to-day? Je sus, the Light of the   world;
4. Come, con-fess Him as your King, Je-sus, the Light of the   world;

Life and mer-cy in   His name, Je-sus,   the Light of the   world.
Send the gos-pel truth to   all,   Je-sus, the Light of the   world.
Go   with truth the nar-row way, Je-sus, the Light of the   world.
Then the bells of heav'n will ring, Je-sus, the Light of the   world.

CHORUS.

We'll walk in the light, beautiful light, Come where the dew-drops of mercy are bright;

Shine all around us by day and by night, Je-sus, the Light of the   world.

No. 20. MISSIONARY BELLS.

COPYRIGHT, 1899, BY WM. J. KIRKPATRICK.
USED BY PER.

E. E. HEWITT.

WM. J. KIRKPATRICK.

1. Keep them ringing, keep them ringing, mis-sion-a-ry bells, Peal-ing
2. Keep them ringing, keep them ringing, let the children's hands Pull the
3. Keep them ringing, keep them ringing, ev-'ry one may share In the

out the news of Je-sus' love; While our gifts we bring to Je-sus,
cords of love and faith and praise, Till the children now in dark-ness,
lov-ing serv-ice of our King; Bring an of-f'ring, will-ing of-f'ring,

hap-py mu-sic swells, Tell-ing of our bless-ed Friend a-bove.
hear of God's commands, Learn to fol-low in the Sav-ior's ways.
wrap it up in pray'r; Help the mis-sion-a-ry bells to ring.

CHORUS.

Bells! bells! mis-sion-a-ry bells, Keep them ringing, keep them ringing,

each a sto-ry tells; Sounding loud and free o-ver land and sea,

Missionary Bells.

Keep them ring-ing, keep them ring-ing, mis-sion - a - ry bells.

No. 21. THE FOUNTAIN OF LIFE.

COPYRIGHT, 1897, BY W. E. M. HACKLEMAN.

J. T. REESE.

1. There is a fountain filled with blood Drawn from Immanuel's veins,
2. The   dy - ing thief re-joiced to see That foun-tain in his day;
3. Thou dy-ing Lamb, Thy precious blood Shall nev-er lose its power,

And sinners, plunged beneath that flood, Lose all their guilty   stains.
And there may I. tho' vile   as he, Wash all my sins a - way.
Till all the ransomed Church of God Be saved, to sin   no more.

CHORUS.

The foun - tain is flowing, Come wash in its waters so free;......
The fountain of life   is flow - ing, Come wash in its waters, its wa-ters so free;

The foun - - tain is flow-ing, Flowing for you and for me.
The foun-tain of life is flow - ing, Flow-ing for you and for me.

No. 22. THE WONDERFUL SAVIOR.

D. C. CARSON. CHAS. H. GABRIEL.

1. I've found a friend, the best of all, Je-sus, the wonderful Sav-ior!
2. With out-cast sin-ners He did eat, Je-sus, the wonderful Sav-ior!
3. For us He suffered want and shame, Je-sus, the wonderful Sav-ior!

He heard my weak, but earnest call, Je-sus, the wonderful Sav-ior!
And wash'd His own dis-ci-ples feet, Je-sus, the wonderful Sav-ior!
We're saved thro' faith in His dear name, Je-sus, the wonderful Sav-ior!

When lost in sin He heard my cry; To earth He came, for me to die; And
Tho' without sin, for us He died; On Cal-v'ry cross was cru-ci-fied; Bu-
No oth-er name for sinners giv'n; No oth-er name in earth or heav'n; But

now He's reigning up on high, Is this wonderful, wonderful Sav-ior.
ried, a - rose and glo - ri - fied, Was this wonderful, wonderful Sav-ior.
all must come, who'd be forgiv'n, To this wonderful, wonderful Sav-ior.

CHORUS.

Wonderful, wonderful Sav-ior! Won-der-ful, won-der-ful Sav-ior!

The Wonderful Savior.

Of Him I'll sing, and ev-er will cling To this wonderful, wonderful Savior.

No. 23.   **NEAR THE CROSS.**

FANNY J. CROSBY.   W. H. DOANE.

1. Je - sus, keep me near the cross, There a pre cious foun - tain,
2. Near the cross, a trem-bling soul, Love and mer - cy found me;
3. Near the cross! O Lamb of God, Bring its scenes be - fore me;
4. Near the cross I'll watch and wait, Hop - ing, trust-ing ev - er,

Free to all— a heal-ing stream, Flows from Cal-v'ry's mountain.
There the bright and Morn-ing Star Shed its beams a-round me.
Help me walk from day to day, With its shad-ows o'er me.
Till I reach the gold-en strand, Just be-yond the riv - er.

CHORUS.

In the cross, in the cross, Be my glo - ry ev - er;

Till my rap - tured soul shall find Rest be-yond the riv - er.

No. 24.   THE GLAD GOOD NEWS.

CHAS. H. GABRIEL.   E. O. EXCELL.

1. "With an ev-er-last-ing love," came the message from a-bove,—
2. Tho' un-mind-ful we have been, and have wandered on in sin,
3. O-pen now to Him your heart, lest for-ev-er He de-part,

"I have loved thee." God hath spoken, tell the news; (the glad good news;)
Still His voice is ev-er speak-ing, tell the news; (the glad good news;)
And ac-cept the gracious blessing, tell the news; (the glad good news;)

Heark-en, soul, un-to His voice, and for-ev-er-more re-joice
He, re-ject-ed o'er and o'er, still is wait-ing at the door,
"With an ev-er-last-ing love," let us each the mes-sage prove,

That His word can-not be bro-ken, tell the news, (the glad good news.)
And thy soul in mer-cy seek-ing, tell the news, (the glad good news.)
And with joy His name con-fess-ing, tell the news, (the glad good news.)

CHORUS.

Tell the news, ... the glad good news, Tell the
Oh, tell the news.   the glad good news,

The Glad Good News.

news......... from shore to shore!..... At the door He waits for thee,
Oh, tell the news   from shore to shore!

Love di-vine His on-ly plea, Tell the news,........ the glad good news.
                                          Oh, tell the news,

No. 25.   JESUS LOVES US ALL.

MAGGIE E. GREGORY.   H. A. HENRY.

1. We are Jesus' little ones! Tho' we're small, very small, Yet we may love and
2. We will listen while we're young, To His call, loving call; We in His steps will
3. Je-sus bears us in His arms, Lest we fall, lest we fall; He dear-ly loves the

REFRAIN.

serve Him too, For Jesus loves us all.)
fol - low on, For Jesus loves us all. } Je-sus loves the children, One and all,
lit - tle ones. Yes, Jesus loves us all.)

great and small; And He has room for us in heav'n, For Jesus loves us all.

No. 26. THE SONG OF JUBILEE.

Mrs. HARRIET E. JONES.　　　　　　　　　　　　　　FRANK M. DAVIS.

1. Sing the Christian's marching song, and sing it with a will;. Let the
2. How the soldiers shouted when they heard the dear old song! How their
3. Yes, and there were loy-al men, whose hearts with joy did swell, As they
4. Let us sing the dear old song, and sing it o'er and o'er; Sing it

mu - sic float a-long o'er val-ley, plain, and hill;　Sing as did the
fa - ces brightened as the mu - sic rolled a - long!　How that song of
bore the flag a - long of Him they loved so well; Blood-stained flag of
with the spir - it of the dear saints gone be-fore,　Sing it thro' our

saints of old—in heav-en singing still, While they were marching to glory.
Jesus helped to make the feeble strong. While they were marching to glory.
One who died that they with Him might dwell, While they were marching to glory.
marchings here, then sing it evermore, While we are marching to glo-ry.

CHORUS.

O sing, O sing the song of jubilee! O sing, O sing of Him who set you free!

Sing of Him each step you take in love and loyalty, While you are marching to glo-ry.

No. 27.   ON THE ROCK.

FRED WOODROW.   C. C. CASE.

1. Standing on the Rock of A - ges, The Rock that shall en-dure, Un-shak-en by
2. Standing on the Rock of A - ges, We view the tranquil soul, Untroubled by
3. Standing on the Rock of A - ges, No need have we to fear, God ban-ish-es

the tem-pest, E - ter-nal, firm and sure; There is a safe re - treat, A
the tem-pest, Or surg-ing billows' roll; Be dangers what they may, And
our sor - row, God wipes a-way our tear; We're watching, we believe, We

refuge strong and free, A-mid the stormy billows Of life's tempestuous sea.
break the waves of care, A-mid the wild com-mo-tion, We stand in safe-ty there.
trust His promise sure, That crowns of joy are wait-ing For all His saints se-cure.

CHORUS.

Stand - - ing, stand - ing, Standing on the Rock of A - ges,

Standing on the Rock, I am standing on the Rock,

Stand - - ing, stand - - ing, No need have I to fear.

Standing on the Rock, I am standing on the Rock,

28 LET NOT YOUR HEART BE TROUBLED.

Mrs. IDA M. BUDD.
DUET for TENOR and ALTO.

CHAS. H. GABRIEL

1. "Let not your heart be troub-led," Oh, words of com-fort sweet! We
2. "Let not your heart be troub-led," Tho' dark the way may be; Cast
3. "Let not your heart be troub-led," For to His glorious home—The

bow, O bless-ed Sav-ior, A - dor-ing at Thy feet; Thy cheering words so
all thy care up-on Him, And He will care for thee. His wisdom still will
place He is pre-par-ing, His own at last shall come. Oh, teach us, lov-ing

ten - der, Our hearts would gladly heed; Our will-ing feet would
guide thee, His lov - ing hand up - hold; His mer - cy keep thee
Sav - ior, To walk the nar-row way; And all a - long the

CHORUS.

fol - low Where'er our Lord shall lead.)
ev - er, Safe. safe with-in His fold. } Let not your heart be troubled, Let
journey, Still may we hear Thee say:)

not your heart be troubled, As ye be-lieve in the Fa-ther, Be -

Owned by Brown Bros., Indianapolis.

Let Not your Heart be Troubled.

lieve in me; Let not your heart be troubled, neither let it be a-

fraid. As ye believe in the Fa - ther, Be - lieve in me.

Rit.

29   JUST AS I AM.

CHARLOTTE ELLIOTT.   WM. B. BRADBURY.

1. Just as I am, with - out one plea, But that Thy blood was shed for me,
2. Just as I am, and waiting not To rid my soul of one dark blot,
3. Just as I am, tho' tossed a - bout With many a conflict, many a doubt,
4. Just as I am—poor, wretched, blind, Sight, rich-es, healing of the mind,
5. Just as I am—Thou wilt receive, Wilt welcome, pardon, cleanse, relieve;
6. Just as I am—Thy love unknown Hath broken ev - 'ry bar-rier down;

And that Thou bidd'st me come to Thee, O Lamb of God, I come! I come!
To Thee whose blood can cleanse each spot, O Lamb of God, I come! I come!
Fightings with - in, and fears without, O Lamb of God, I come! I come!
Yea, all I need, in Thee to find, O Lamb of God, I come! I come!
Be - cause Thy prom-ise I be-lieve, O Lamb of God, I come! I come!
Now, to be Thine, yea, Thine a-lone, O Lamb of God, I come! I come!

No. 30.   VICTORY.

ADA BLENKHORN.   CHAS. H. GABRIEL.

1. On-ward, the foe to meet, fear-less we go;   Je - sus, our Captain,
2. Clad in the armor bright, God doth provide Breast-plate and helmet.
3. See, see the mighty host Strong on the field! Shout, for the Lord shall

leads the way! Strong is His mighty arm, faithful and true, Trusting in
shield and sword, Bravely we face the foe, bold-ly we cry— Vic-t'ry is
make us free! Let our ho-san-nas ring loud-ly and long, To Him who

CHORUS.

Him we'll win the day. }
ours thro' Christ the Lord. } Then we'll march on to vic - to - ry, march, a
gives the vic - to - ry. }

happy throng; March on to vic - to-ry, valiant, brave, and strong! Hark! hark! the

bat-tle-cry sounds above our song—Vic-to-ry! vic-to-ry! vic - to - ry!

No. 31.   LEAVE IT TO HIM.

Rev. J. E. Rankin.   Chas. H. Gabriel.

1. Why go a - round with troub - led soul! There's One that makes the
2. How - ev - er man thy lot may slight, He'll turn to day thy
3. How - ev - er dark thy path may be, Dark and un - scrut - a -
4. Sure He who sets the mount - ain fast, When all earth's clouds are

wound - ed whole; Up - on the Lord thy bur - den roll:—
dark - est night, And flood from heav'n thy path with light,
ble to thee, He rules on high your des - ti - ny,—
driv - en past, Will jus - ti - fy His ways at last,

Leave it to Him,   Leave it to Him............
Leave it to Him,   Leave it to Him.

FINE.

CHORUS.

Leave it to Him............ who knoweth all,............. Him who
Leave it to Him who knoweth all, Leave it to Him,

D.S.

marks...... the sparrow's fall,..... Who list - ens to the raven's call,
Leave it to Him who marks the sparrow's fall,

No. 32. THE SWORD OF THE LORD.

Mrs. FRANK A. BRECK.

GRANT C. TULLAR.

1. A - rise!   a - rise!   a-rise! be not a-fraid; A - rise!   a-
2. March on! march on!   for God is with the right; March on! march
3. Be - hold!   be - hold!   O trust-ing lit - tle band; Be - hold!   be-

A-rise!   a-rise!   A-rise!

rise! for God will be thine aid: Yea, the Lord will go before thee. And His
on!   and ye shall surely smite, As a man, the host of Mid-ian, For the
hold! and ye shall understand: Tho' the evil foes surround thee, Yet they

a-rise!

banner shall be o'er thee, While the mighty pow'r of e-vil shall be stayed.
Lord will fight for Gideon. And the army of thy foes   be   put   to flight.
never shall confound thee, If ye faithfully o - bey   the Lord's command.

CHORUS.

Trust ye in the Lord forever, And thy trust He will reward; He will be thy strong de-

liv-'rer, He will be thy watch and ward: With "the sword of the Lord and Gid-eon,"

The Sword of the Lord.

Ye shall smite the host of Mid-ian; Ye shall con-quer in the bat - tle, Praise the Lord!

No. 33. LO! I AM WITH YOU.

Mrs. J. V. C.   Matt. 28: 20.   Mrs. J. V. Coombs.

1. Hear the words of long a - go, From the mount in Gal - i - lee,
2. See the hea - then na-tions bow, As they catch the ray of light,
3. Loud and strong the cry comes on, To us as to those of old,

Spok-en by the Lord of love, 'Teach the world to fol - low me."
Ea - ger now to be released From the dark ness of the night.
"Teach the world to fol - low me," Let the sto - ry oft be told.

Chorus.

Lo! I am with you, Lo! I am with you,

Lo! I am with you al - ways Ev - en to the end.

No. 34. ON TO THE BATTLE.

LIZZIE DE ARMOND.   CHAS. H. GABRIEL.

1. On to the bat - tle, O sol - dier of Je - sus, Forth to the
2. Mil- lions are dy - ing! go, res - cue the cap-tives From sin's pol -
3. On! Sa - tan's ter - rors shall not o - ver-whelm you; Stand up for

con - flict, the war - fare be - gin! Pow - ers of dark-ness a -
lu - tion! re - joice in His grace! Foes with - out num- ber may
Je - sus! His trust ne'er be-tray; For - ward! the watch-fires now

round you are pressing. Raise on high your standard, the faith-ful shall win.
sore - ly dis-tress you; Boldly strug-gle on in the light of His face.
gleam on the mountains, Christ, your light and strength, goes before all the way.

CHORUS.

Shout! for the Mighty, the Lord ev - er - last- ing, Calls you to

vic - to - ry; why fear the hosts of sin? Glad-ness, like morning, shall

On to the Battle.

break o'er the hill-tops, Glo-ry,hal-le- lu - jah! a crown you shall win.

No. 35.   NEARER, MY GOD, TO THEE.

QUARTETTE.

Mrs. S. F. Adams.   COPYRIGHT, 1897, BY W. E. M. HACKLEMAN.   W. E. M. Hackleman.

1. Near - er, my God, to Thee, Near - er to Thee! E'en tho' it
2. Tho' like a wan-der-er, The sun gone down, Dark - ness be
3. There let the way ap-pear Steps un - to heav'n; All that Thou
4. Or   if, on joy-ful wing, Cleav-ing the sky, Sun, moon.and

be   a cross That rais-eth me; Still all my songs shall be—
o - ver me, My rest a stone;- Yet in my dreams I'd be—
send-est me, In mer - cy given; An - gels to beck - on me
stars for-got, Up - ward I fly, Still all my song shall be,

p Rit. ad lib.

Near-er, my God, to Thee! Nearer,my God,to Thee.Nearer to Thee!
Near-er, my God, to Thee! Nearer,my God.to Thee,Nearer to Thee!
Near-er, my God,to Thee! Nearer,my God,to Thee,Nearer to Thee!
Near-er, my God,to Thee! Nearer,my God,to Thee, Nearer to Thee!

No. 36. UNDER THE BANNER OF LOVE.

Words by Isaac Naylor.

1. Look! look! the foe is must'ring his host in proud ar - ray,
2. To arms! to arms! ye com - rades, the trump-et blast rings out!
3. Your swords all drawn and sharp-ened, your ar - mor glist'ning bright,
4. The troops of dark - ness fal - ter, their flag falls to the ground!
5. Our Cap - tain, all vic - to - rious, in ar-mor bright and strong,
6. And when the fight is fin - ished, we'll put our hel-met down,

Their ar - mor tight - ly gird - ing, pre - par - ing for the fray;
The foes of truth now block-ade our forts all round a - bout;
Strike hard and strong, and no - bly, for God, and truth, and right;
From Calv'ry's sa - cred al - tar, rings triumph's joy - ful sound:
Has led His church all - glo - rious a - gainst the a - lien throng;
Our ar - mor bright and bur-nished for heav - en's robe and crown;

The bat - tle cry has sound - ed, their ban - ners flut-ter out,
E - quip! E - quip! brave sol - diers, up! up! and face the foe!
The smoke of war may dark - en, the clash of arms be loud,
The foes, dis-mayed and conquered, in ter - ror quit the field;
He'll lead un - til all na - tions in ad - o - ra - tion bring
The strife and strug - gle o - ver, the din hushed by the song,

Our forts are all sur - round-ed! hark! hear the enemy's shout! ⎫
Stand firm, fear not, nor fal - ter! all armed, to bat - tle go! ⎪
But Sa - tan's host must slack - en be-fore the brave and proud. ⎬ Oh!
Our roy - al Prince is hon - ored, as Sa-tan's ar-mies yield! ⎪
Their hom-age, tro - phies, prais - es, and crown Him as their King. ⎪
With Christ we'll reign for - ev - er amid the white-robed throng. ⎭

Under the Banner of Love.

CHORUS.

Un-der the banner of love we'll fight our way to glo-ry! Un-der the banner of love we'll conquer or we'll die! Un-der the banner of love we'll spread the gospel story; Our Je-sus and sal-va-tion shall be our battle cry.

No. 37.   COME, THOU FOUNT.

Rev. R. Robinson

John Wyeth   FINE.

1. Come, Thou fount of ev-'ry bless-ing, Tune my heart to sing Thy grace;
{ Streams of mer-cy, nev-er ceas-ing, Call for songs of loud-est praise;

D.C.—Praise the mount—I'm fixed upon it! Mount of Thy re-deem-ing love.

D. C.

Teach me some mel-o-dious son-net, Sung by flam-ing tongues a-bove;

2 Here I'll raise my Ebenezer,
   Hither by Thy help I'm come;
And I hope, by Thy good pleasure,
   Safely to arrive at home:
Jesus sought me when a stranger,
   Wandering from the fold of God;
He, to rescue me from danger,
   Interposed His precious blood.

3 Oh, to grace how great a debtor,
   Daily I'm constrained to be!
Let Thy goodness, as a fetter,
   Bind my wandering heart to Thee;
Prone to wander, Lord, I feel it—
   Prone to leave the God I love—
Here's my heart, oh, take and seal it,
   Seal it for Thy courts above.

No. 38. SEEK JESUS TO-DAY.

IDA M. BUDD. CHAS. H. GABRIEL.

1. Soul, wake from thy sleep-ing, Thy vig-il be keep-ing!
2. Hark! how He's en-treat-ing, Love's prom-ise re-peat-ing;
3. Earth tempts thee with pleas-ure, Christ of-fers thee treas-ure,

Mists round thee are creep-ing. Swift com-eth the night.
Time swift-ly is fleet-ing. Soul, turn not a-way.
Gifts rich be-yond meas-ure, What wilt thou de-cide?

Why aim-less-ly drift-ing Where shad-ows are shift-ing?
Lo! hath He not told thee His grace shall en-fold thee?
Wilt thou not a-dore Him, Bow low-ly be-fore Him.

See! yon-der up-lift-ing Gates ra-diant with light.
His might shall up-hold thee, O seek Him to-day!
And meek-ly im-plore Him With thee to a-bide?

CHORUS.

Seek...... Him to-day...... Make..... no de-
Seek Him to-day, Seek Him to-day, Make no de-lay,

Seek Jesus To-Day.

lay,......... He waits to re - ceive thee, From guilt to re-
make no de - lay,

lieve thee; He will not de-ceive thee, O seek Him to - day!

No. 39. MORE LOVE TO THEE.

ELIZABETH PRENTIS. W. H. DOANE.

1. More love to Thee, O Christ; More love to Thee; Hear Thou the
2. Once earth-ly joy I craved Sought peace and rest; Now Thee a-
3. Then shall my lat - est breath, Whis-per Thy praise, This be the

pray'r, I make on bend-ed knee; This is my earn-est plea,
lone I seek, Give what is best; This all my pray'r shall be,
part - ing cry My heart shall raise; This still its pray'r shall be,

More love, O Christ, to Thee, More love to Thee; More love to Thee.
More love, O Christ, to Thee, More love to Thee; More love to Thee.
More love, O Christ, to Thee, More love to Thee; More love to Thee.

No. 40.   PRAISE THE LORD.

Rev. F. L. SNYDER.   GEO. E. MYERS.

1. "From the ris - ing of the sun un-til the go - ing down thereof,"
2. From the ris - ing of the sun un-til the gath'ring shades of night,
3. From the ris . ing of the sun un-til its rays are seen no more,

Praise the Lord,   Praise the Lord,   For the
Praise the Lord,   Praise the Lord,   For the
Praise the Lord,   Praise the Lord,   When our

Praise the Lord,   Praise the Lord,

ran - som of His Son, O wondrous, wondrous gift of love, Praise the
grace that helps you triumph o - ver wrong and for the right, Praise the
tri - als all are end - ed and we meet on yonder shore, Praise the

CHORUS.

Lord,   Praise the Lord. Praise the Lord,   with the
Lord,   Praise the Lord.
Lord,   Praise the Lord.

Praise the Lord,   Praise the Lord,

fullness of your soul, Praise the Lord, For the grace that's made you whole, Hal-le-

Prais the Lord,

Praise the Lord.

lu - - jah! Hal-le - lu - - jah! Praise the Lord. praise the Lord.
lujah to His name, Hal-le - lu-jah to His name, Praise the Lord,

No. 41. NEARER HOME.

J. T. REESE.

DUET. *Slowly and with expression.*

1. One sweet-ly sol-emn thought Comes to me o'er and o'er,—
2. I'm near-er my Fa-ther's house, Where heav'nly mansions be;
3. I'm near-er the bound of life, Where we lay our bur-dens down;

I'm near-er my home to - day Than ev-er I've been be - fore.
I'm near-er the great white throne; Near-er the Jas-per sea.
I'm near-er the time to leave The cross, and wear the crown.

CHORUS.

I'm near - - er my beau-ti-ful home, I'm near - - er my
I'm near-er my home, I'm near-er my home,

beautiful home, I'm nearer my home in heav'n to-day Than ever I've been before.

No. 42.   SUNSHINE BY AND BY.

Mrs. L. M. Beal Bateman.   Chas. H. Gabriel.

1. There are clouds, but high above them Shines undimmed the faithful sun;
2. Dark - est clouds have sil-ver lin - ings, E - ven though no shin-ing rim
3. Do not droop and sigh and question, Grop ing on in doubt and fear;
4. Nev - er mind how dark it may be, How the winds may threat'ning cry;

Then look up; it may be bright-er Long, be - fore the day is done.
May ap-pear to clos - er vis - ion, Weak and oft by tears made dim.
Look a - loft! a - bove the mountain See the rainbow arch ap-pear.
Lift your eyes, and trust His prom-ise, Your re-demp-tion draw-eth nigh!

CHORUS.

Do not lin - - - ger in the shad - - ows, Your re-
Do not lin - ger in the shadows, Do not lin - ger in the shadows, Your re-

demp - tion draw-eth nigh; There are bright - - er
demption draweth nigh, your redemption draweth nigh; There are brighter days in waiting,

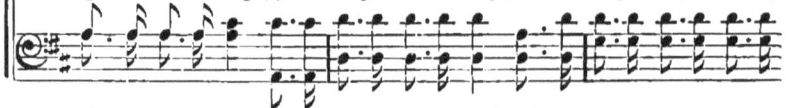

days in wait - ing, There'll be sunshine by and by............
there are brighter days in waiting, There'll be sunshine, There'll be sunshine by and by

Sunshine By and By.

There'll be sun - - - shine, blessed sun - - - shine When the
There'll be sunshine by and by, bless-ed sunshine by and by, When the

mists have roll'd a - way;.......... There'll be sun - - - shine,
mists have roll'd, when the mists have roll'd away; There'll be sunshine by and by,

bless-ed sun - - shine, When the mists have roll'd a - way.
bless-ed sunshine by and by,

No. 43. O FOR A HEART.

C. WESLEY.   S. WEBBE.

1. O for a heart to praise my God, A heart from sin set free;—
2. A heart resigned, sub-mis - sive, meek, My great Re-deem-er's throne;
3. O for a low - ly con - trite heart, Be-liev - ing, true and clean;
4. A heart in ev -'ry thought renewed, And full of love di - vine;

A heart that al-ways feels Thy blood, So free - ly shed for me:—
Where on - ly Christ is heard to speak,—Where Je-sus reigns a - lone.
Which neither life nor death can part From Him that dwells within:—
Per - fect, and right, and pure, and good, A cop - y, Lord, of Thine.

No. 44. HAVE FAITH IN GOD.

E. E. HEWITT.   GEO. F. ROSCHE.

DUET.

1. "Have faith in God," the Sav - ior said: He saw the path that we must
2. Have faith in God tho' clouds a - rise And o - ver-spread the glowing
3. Have faith in God: A fa-ther's heart Would to his child all good im-
4. Have faith in God: His word di-vine By day and night shall brightly

tread; The frequent thorn, the fading flow'r, The joy or pain of ev-'ry hour.
skies; Tho' sun and stars grow dim and pale, His boundless love shall never fail
part; Much more will He regard the pray'r Of those who cast on Him their care.
shine, Un-til we pass the gates of light And faith shall yield to blissful sight.

CHORUS.

O bless - ed faith! Its song of cheer Re-vives our
          O faith!   of cheer
The Shep-herd's staff,   The Shep-herd's rod,   [Omit........
        the staff,   the rod,

hope, dis-pels our fear;
our hope,   our fear;
.........................] Still leads us on; have faith in God.
                         in God.

No. 45. COME AND REST.

J. BARNBY.

pp

1. "Come and rest, come and rest," Je - sus now calls to thee;
2. Sweet and low, sweet and low, Comes His dear voice to thee;
3. Come to - day, come to - day, Rest in the Sav - ior's love;

"Rest, rest on my breast," Call - eth He ten - der - ly.
Now, now, hear him now, Call - ing so lov - ing - ly.
Al - ways with him stay— Dwelling with Him in love.

mf   *pp*

"Come, take my yoke, 'tis bond - age blest; Come, heav - y la - dened
Fear not the storms of life that blow, Nor the wild waves that
Wea - ry ones, come with - out de - lay, Nev - er a - gain from

and dis - tressed. And I will make you free;
break and flow; In - to His arms now flee.
Him to stray; Here His great mer - cy prove,

p   *rall e dim.*   *pp*

Come, ye wea - ry ones, come, ye la - dened ones, rest..........
He, His lov - ing ones, He, His trust - ing ones, keep.........
Here so peace - ful - ly, here, so sweet - ly to rest..........

No. 46.   VICTORY!

C. H. G.   CHAS. H. GABRIEL.

1, Hap - py in the Sav - ior we are marching on to glo - ry,
2. Clouds and dark-ness, sin and er - ror—see them dis - ap-pear-ing.
3. Faith will bring the vic - to - ry! re-joice, the day is break-ing!

Sing - ing hal - le - lu - jah to the Lamb of Cal - va - ry!
As   the hosts of   Is - ra - el   ad - vance in proud ar - ray;
Floods of gold - en   glo - ry_ now il - lum - i - nate the sky;

All   a - long the way to oth - ers tell - ing out the sto - ry—
Hark! the bu - gle notes of the mil - len - ni - um is near - ing,
Might - y songs of tri-umph from the Ba - bel din a - wak - ing.

"Je - sus lives, He lives! be-hold the year of ju - bi - lee."
Glo - ry hal - le - lu - jah! let us watch, and fight, and pray!
Her - ald now the glo - ry that is com - ing by and by.

CHORUS.

Praise Him! Praise Him! Beau - ti - ful strains of mu-sic bring;
Praise Him in the high - est, glo - ry!

Victory!

Praise Him! Praise Him! Love and a-dore the King!
Praise Him! tell the won-drous sto-ry!

for-ev-er!

Praise Him! Praise Him! Let the re-deemed of
Praise Him! wave His ban-ner o'er Thee,

Zi-on sing Un-til all the world shall know and love the Lord.

No. 47. FROM EVERY STORMY WIND.

1. From ev-'ry storm-y wind that blows, From ev-'ry swelling tide of woes,
2. There is a place where Je-sus sheds The oil of gladness on our heads,
3. There is a scene where spir-its blend, Where friend holds fellow-ship with friend;
4. Ah! whith-er could we flee for aid, When tempted, des-o-late, dismayed;
5. There, there on eagle wings we soar, And sin and sense mo-lest no more;
6. Oh! let my hand for-get her skill, My tongue be si-lent, cold and still,

There is a calm, a sure re-treat;'Tis found be-neath the mer-cy-seat.
A place than all be-side more sweet; It is the blood-bought mer-cy-seat.
Tho' sundered far, by faith they meet Around one common mer-cy-seat.
Or how the hosts of hell de-feat, Had suf-f'ring saints no mer-cy-seat.
And heav'n comes down our souls to greet, While glory crowns the mer-cy-seat.
This bounding heart forget to beat, Ere I for-get the mer-cy-seat.

No. 48. HIS PROMISES ARE TRUE.

Helen Dungan.

J. M. Dungan.

DUET.

1. When o'er my path the clouds hang thick and dark, When hope is gone, and doubts my
2. They nev-er fail, tho' earth may pass away, And earthly friends to me may
3. O blessed Word, be Thou my shield and guide While life shall last, and succor

way obscure, Help me, O Lord, to look a-bove the gloom; To trust Thy
prove untrue; There is a Friend whose mercy fail-eth not; I'll trust His
strong and sure; And when at last I reach my home a-bove, I'll test Thy

CHORUS.

prom-is-es, for they are sure. Yes, they are sure,......they will en-
prom-is-es, for they are true.
prom-is-es, they will en-dure. Yes, they are sure,

dure,........ Tho' tri-als dark........ my way ob-scure;........
they will endure, Tho' tri-als dark my way obscure;

My home a-bove,....... God's gift of love,........ I'll gain at
My home a-bove, God's gift of love,

His Promises are True.

last;.............. last; His word is sure.

I'll gain at last;

His word is sure.

No. 49.   # PRAISE THE LORD.

J. KEMPTHORNE.

LOWELL MASON.

1. Praise the Lord; ye heav'ns, adore Him; Praise Him, angels in the height;
2. Praise the Lord, for He hath spoken; Worlds His mighty voice o-beyed;
3. Praise the Lord, for He is glo-rious; Nev-er shall His promise fail;
4. Praise the God of our sal-va-tion; Hosts on high, His pow'r proclaim;

Sun and moon, rejoice before Him; Praise Him, all ye stars of light.
Laws which never shall be broken. For their guidance He hath made.
God hath made His saints victorious; Sin and death shall not prevail.
Heav'n and earth, and all creation, Laud and magnify His name.

Sun   and moon, rejoice before Him; Praise   Him, all ye stars of light.

Hal - le - lu - jah! A - men,   A - men, A - - - men.

A - men, Hal - le - lu - jah! A - men, A - men, A - men.

No. 50. WE SHALL UNDERSTAND.

Mrs. M. A. Holt.   Chas. H. Gabriel.

1. When the shad-ows change to sun-light, And we see with clear-er eye;
2. When we gath - er fade-less flow - ers, Where no frosts are ev - er known
3. When we list - en to the mus - ic, That so strangely thrills the soul,
4. We shall sure - ly see here - af - ter How each heart-ache and each sob,

When there are no clouds to dark - en The bright blue of sum-mer sky,
And the winds of sad No-vem - ber Nev - er 'round our pathway moan,
Growing sweet-er while the a - ges On - ward in their glo - ry roll,
Lift - ed up our wounded spir - its Near - er to the bless-ed God.

We shall smile at all the sor - row That has vexed our spir - its here,
In the glow of Spring E-ter - nal, We shall sure - ly un - der-stand
In those ho - ly peace - ful mo-ments We may be sur-prised to know
We shall un - der-stand for - ev - er, All the mys - ter - ies of earth,

When we un - der-stand the mean-ing Of the earth-cross and the tear.
How a lov - ing Fa - ther led us Thro' a dark and wea - ry land.
That the mel - o - dy of heav - en Was a - wak-ened here be-low.
And at last shall know each tri - al, Was a gem of un - told worth.

We Shall Understand.

We shall un - der-stand,   We shall un - der-stand,
sure - ly un - der-stand,   sure - ly un - der-stand

We shall un - der-stand the mean-ing by and by,............
by and by,

When the cares of life are o'er, On that bright e - ter - nal shore,

We shall un - der-stand the mean-ing by and by............
by and by.

No. 51. WORK, FOR THE NIGHT IS COMING.

1 Work for the night is coming,
  Work thro' the morning hours.
Work while the dew is sparkling;
  Work mid springing flowers;
Work when the day grows brighter,
  Work in the glowing sun;
Work, for the night is coming,
  When man's work is done.

1 Work, for the night is coming,
  Work thro' the sunny noon;
Fill brightest hours with labor.
  Rest comes sure and soon;

Give every flying moment
  Something to keep in store;
Work, for the night is coming,
  When man works no more.

3 Work, for the night is coming,
  Under the sunset skies;
While their bright tints are glowing,
  Work, for daylight flies;
Work till the last beam fadeth,
  Fadeth to shine no more;
Work while the night is darkening,
  When man's work is o'er.

No. 52. WILL THERE BE ANY STARS?

E. E. HEWITT.   JNO. R. SWENEY.

1. I am thinking to-day of that beau-ti-ful land I shall reach when the
2. In the strength of the Lord let me labor and pray, Let me watch as a
3. O' what joy it will be when His face I behold, Living gems at His

sun goeth down; When thro' wonderful grace by my Sav-ior I stand, Will there
win-ner of souls; That bright stars may be mine in the glo-ri-ous day When His
feet to lay down; It would sweeten my bliss in the cit-y of gold, Should there

CHORUS.

be an-y stars in my crown? }
praise like the sea billow rolls. } Will there be any stars, any stars in my crown?
be an-y stars in my crown? }

When at evening the sun go-eth down?......When I wake with the blest
go-eth down?

In the mansions of rest, Will there be an-y stars in my crown?......
an-y stars in my crown?

No. 53. JESUS IS CALLING TO-DAY.

CHARLOTTE G. HOMER.　　　　　　　　　　Dr. L. O. EMERSON.

1. Je - sus is call-ing! O hear Him to - day, Call-ing for you,
2. Je - sus is call-ing! Your serv-ice He needs, Call-ing for you,
3. Je - sus is call-ing! He stands at the door, Call-ing for you,

call-ing for you; Will you not quickly the summons o - bey?
call-ing for you; Ten-der - ly, pa - tient-ly with you He pleads,
call-ing for you; O - pen your heart, and His mer-cy im - plore,

CHORUS.

Je-sus is call-ing for you! . . . Call - - ing for you . . . .
for you. Je - sus is call-ing, is call-ing for you,

call - - ing for you, Hear Him to - day—do not
Je - sus is call-ing, is call-ing for you,

turn Him a - way, Je - sus is call-ing for you. . . .
for you,

No. 54. TO ALL MEN EVERYWHERE.

IDA M. BUDD, CHAS. H. GABRIEL.

1. The Lord has need of work-ers to till His vine-yard wide; A -
2. The souls of men are fam-ished, they hun-ger to be fed; Will
3. To souls in bondage groan-ing and long-ing to be free; Christ

far His call is sounding now, why i - dle still a - bide? Go,
you not break, for Je-sus' sake to them the liv - ing bread? Go
bids you speak His message sweet of life and lib - er - ty; To

join the host who serve Him—their pa - tient la - bors share, Pro-
in His strength and shun not His coun-sels to de-clare With
hearts with sor-row break-ing, the news He bids you bear Of

D. S.— *O hast-en to de-clare, Of*

claim - ing His sal - va - tion to all men ev - 'ry - where.
all its hope and warn - ing to all men ev - 'ry - where.
ten - der con - so - la - tion to all men ev - 'ry - where.

per - fect, free sal - va - tion, to all men ev - 'ry - where.

CHORUS.

To all..........men, to all..........men Tell out the joy and
To all men ev-'ry-where The glorious tidings bear,

To All Men Everywhere.

glad-ness that all the world may share, The word the Lord hath spoken,

No. 55. I NEED THEE EVERY HOUR.

Mrs. Annie Hawk.

Robert Lowry.

1. I need Thee ev-'ry hour, Most gracious Lord; No ten-der voice like
2. I need Thee ev-'ry hour, Stay Thou near by; Temptations lose their
3. I need Thee ev-'ry hour, Teach me Thy will; And Thy rich prom-is-
4. I need Thee ev-'ry hour, Most Ho - ly One; O, make me Thine in-

Refrain.

Thine Can peace af - ford.
power When Thou art nigh.
es In me ful - fil.
deed, Thou bless - ed Son.

I need Thee, O, I need Thee,

Ev-'ry hour I need Thee; O, bless me now, my Savior; I come to Thee.

No. 56. HARVEST TIME.

W. A. S. Rev. W. A. Spencer, D. D.

1. The seed I have scattered in spring-time with weeping, And watered with
2. An - oth - er may reap what in spring-time I've planted, An-oth - er re -
3. The thorns will have choked, and the summer sun blasted The most of the

tears and with dews from on high; An - oth - er may shout when the
joice in the fruit of my pain,—Not know-ing my tears when in
seed which in spring-time I've sown; But the Lord who has watched while my

har - vest-ers reap-ing Shall gath-er my grain in the "sweet by and by."
sum- mer I faint-ed While toiling sad-heart-ed in sunshine and rain.
wea - ry toil last - ed Will give me a har vest for what I have done.

CHORUS.

O - ver and o - ver, yes, deep - er and deep-er My heart is pierced

thro' with life's sor-row-ing cry, But the tears of the sow - er and

Harvest Time.

FINE.

songs of the reap-er Shall min - gle to - geth-er in joy by and by.

D. S.

By and by,.... by and by,.... By and by.... by and by..... Yes, the
By and by, by and by, By and by, by and by,

No. 57. IN THE SHADOW OF THE ROCK.

J. V. COOMBS.   J. T. REESE.

SOLO or DUET.

1. In a drear - 'y land I wan-der, And with falt'ring steps I walk;
2. Let me go where my Re-deem-er Has prepared for me sweet rest;
3. So with pa-tient faith I'll wander, And with lov-ing heart I'll walk;
4. Let me go, my soul is wea-ry Of the chains which rudely mock;

But I'll soon be rest-ing yon-der In the shad-ow of the Rock.
In the gold-en home up yon-der, To the mansions of the blest.
I will soon be rest-ing yon-der In the shad-ow of the Rock.
I'll be rest - ing o - ver yon-der In the shad-ow of the Rock.

CHORUS.

In the shad - ow of the Rock, In the shad - ow of the Rock;

I will soon be rest-ing yon-der, In the shad- ow of the Rock.

No. 58.   BE CAREFUL.

C. H. G.   Chas. H. Gabriel.

1. Lit - tle feet, be ver - y care - ful where you go, (where you go,)
2. Lit - tle hands, be ver - y care - ful what you do, (what you do,)
3. Lit - tle eyes, be ver - y care - ful—look a-head, (straight ahead,)
4. Lit - tle ears, be ver - y care - ful what you hear, (what you hear,)
5. Lit - tle hear, tsbe ver - y care - ful to be true, (pure and true,)

As in life you dai - ly trav - el to and fro, (to and fro;)
Wrong or tho't - less ac - tions you will sure - ly rue, (you will rue;)
There are dan - gers in the path our feet must tread, (dai - ly tread;)
When the temp-ter whis - pers to you, dan-ger's near, (ver - ry near;)
Love the Lord and he will sure - ly care for you, (care for you;)

Nev - er for a mo-ment stray from the straight and narrow way,
In - to mis-chief nev - er go, for 'tis ver - y wrong you know,
Then a faith - ful pi - lot be—turn from ev -'ry wrong you see,
Tho' he prom-ise ev -'ry - thing,—ev - ry prom-ise is a sting,
Je - sus will not en - ter in where there is the least of sin.

FINE.

Oh, be care - ful, be care - ful, lit - tle feet.
Oh, be care - ful, be care - ful, lit - tle hands.
Oh, be care - ful, be care - ful, lit - tle eyes.
Oh, be care - ful, be care - ful, lit - tle ears.
Oh, be care - ful, be care - ful, lit - tle hearts.

Be Careful.

CHORUS.

Be care - ful, lit - tle feet, Je - sus watches from a - bove, He
Be care - ful, lit - tle hands, Je - sus watches from a - bove, He
Be care - ful, lit - tle eyes, Je - sus watches from a - bove, He
Be care - ful, lit - tle ears, Je - sus watches from a - bove, He
Be care - ful, lit - tle hearts, Je - sus watches from a - bove, He

D. S.

watch - es o - ver you in tend'rest love, (in ten - der love.)

No. 59. THE LIFE, THE TRUTH, THE WAY.

IDA M. BUDD.   DR. S. B. JACKSON.

1. { Do we want to go to heav'n Land of end-less day?
   { Here's the light that He has given. Je - sus is the....... Way.
2. { Would we grace and wis - dom find In our ear - ly youth?
   { Let the Sav - ior guide our minds. Je - sus is the....... Truth.
3. { Would we live e - ter - nal - ly, Far from sin and strife?
   { Christ from death can set us free—Je - sus is the......... Life.

CHORUS.

Je - sus is the Way, The Truth and the Life,
He will bring us safe - - ly (Omit................)Home to God.

COPYRIGHT, 1898, BY CHAS. H. GABRIEL

No. 60.   LET ME SING THE STORY.

E. A. H.   Rev. E. A. Hoffman.

1. Have you ev-er heard the sto-ry,—Wondrous sweet it is to me,
2. Do you know this mighty Sav-ior, Have you felt His sav-ing pow'r?
3. Was there ev-er such a Sav-ior? Was there ev-er such a Friend?
4. Love, O love this dear Re-deem-er! Cov-e-nant His child to be;

How the Lord of life and glo-ry For the world's redemption died on
He is a-ble now to help you,—To re-new and cleanse your heart this
Was there ev-er such an-oth-er Read-y in the time of need His
And from henceforth follow ful-ly Je-sus Christ, the sin-less Man of

Chorus.

Cal-va-ry?   Let me sing it, Sing the wondrous sto-ry,
ver-y hour.
aid to lend.
Cal-va-ry.

Giv-ing Je-sus all the praise and glo-ry! He's my Sav-ior.
For He is my Sav-ior,

Let Me Sing the Story.

bless-ed be His name, And I will for-ev-er-more His love proclaim.

No. 61. SHALL WE GATHER AT THE RIVER.

R. L.

ROBERT LOWRY. By per.

1. Shall we gath-er at the riv-er, Where bright an-gel feet have trod,
2. On the mar-gin of the riv-er, Wash-ing up its sil-ver spray,
3. On the bo-som of the riv-er, Where the Sav-ior King we own,
4. Soon we'll reach the shining river, Soon our pil-grim-age will cease;

With its crys-tal tide for-ev-er Flow-ing by the throne of God?
We shall walk and wor-ship ev-er. All the hap-py, gold-en day.
We shall meet and sor-row nev-er, 'Neath the glo-ry of the throne.
Soon our hap-py hearts will quiver, With the mel-o-dy of peace.

CHORUS.

Yes, we'll gath-er at the riv-er, The beau-ti-ful, the beau-ti-ful riv-er,

Gath-er with the saints at the riv-er That flows by the throne of God.

No. 62.   WE ARE LITTLE SOLDIERS.

GORA. E. HOWES.   CHAS. H. GABRIEL.

1. We are lit - tle sol - diers, Fight - ing for our king;
2. Sa - tan will en - trap us, If we don't look out;
3. We are lit - tle sol - diers, But we know the right;

Don't you love to hear us, As we so glad - ly sing?
When we see him com - ing, We raise our ar - my shout.
When the foe is near us, We pray, and sing with might.

CHORUS.

Tramp, tramp, tramp, we are com-ing, com-ing, com-ing! Tramp, tramp, tramp, coming

with an ar - my strong;   Tramp, tramp, tramp, we are coming, coming,
we're coming!

com-ing, com-ing, Fighting ev-'ry thing that's wrong. . . . .
Yes,   ev - 'ry thing that's wrong!

No. 63.   SOME BLESSED DAY.

Rev. Johnson Oatman, Jr.   Dr. S. B. Jackson.

1. A few more tears of grief may fall, Before we hear the Savior's call;
2. What tho' the way be rough and dark, God's hand will guide our trembling bark;
3. Our loved and lost of years gone by, Now wait for us   beyond the sky;
4. So we will trust and do our best, Till God shall call us home to rest,

God's hand will wipe them all a - way, Some blessed day, some blessed day.
Thro' stormy wave, o'er ocean's foam, Some blessed day we'll reach our home.
Some blessed day we'll reach that shore To live with them for-ev - er - more.
Then we will go with Him to stay, Some blessed day, some blessed day.

CHORUS.

Some bless-ed day........ we will re - joice,.......When we shall
Some blessed day,   yes,   we will rejoice,

bear........ the Savior's voice;......"Come home, my child!"....
When we shall hear, hear   the Savior's voice;   "Come home, my child!"

we'll hear Him say,........Some blessed day,........some blessed day.
we'll hear Him say,   Some blessed day,

No. 64. CHRIST HAS COME TO REIGN.

CHARLOTTE G. HOMER.   CHAS. H. GABRIEL.

1. Praise Him! praise Him! Car - ol a song of glo - ry!
2. Praise Him! praise Him! Beau - ti - ful car - ols bring - ing,
3. Praise Him! praise Him! Tell of His grace a-bound - ing!

Tell of the won - ders of His love; Tell of the man -sions
Un - to His name the choic - est give, For He was slain that
Tell of His mer - cy, rich and free; Tell of His death on

bright a-bove; Sweet -ly! sweet-ly! Ech - o the Gos - pel sto - ry,
we might live! Tell it! tell it! Set the glad bells a - ring-ing;
Cal - va - ry; Sing it! sing it! Un - til the hills re-sound-ing,

Shout-ing a - loud the glad re-frain,"Christ has come to reign!"
Her-ald it o - ver land and main,"Christ has come to reign!"
Ech - o the glad triumphant strain,"Christ has come to reign!"

CHORUS.

Let the mer - ry, mer - ry bells, Ech - o the joy - ful song;

joy - ful song;

Christ Has Come To Reign.

For of life and love it tells Un - to the bus - y throng.

Let the si - lent rocks and hills An-swer in glad ac-claim,
in glad ac-claim,

While the vales and sing-ing rills, Car - ol the Sav-ior's name.
bless-ed name.

No. 65.   AM I A SOLDIER.

ISAAC WATTS.   THOS. A. ARNE.

1. Am I a sol - dier of the cross, A foll-'wer of the Lamb,
2. Must I be car - ried to the skies On flow-'ry beds of ease,
3. Are there no foes for me to face? Must I not stem the flood?
4. Sure I must fight, if I would reign; Increase my cour-age, Lord;

And shall I fear to own His cause, Or blush to speak His name?
While oth-ers fought to win the prize, And sailed thro' blood-y seas?
Is this vile world a friend to grace, To help me on to God?
I'll bear the toil, en - dure the pain, Sup - port - ed by Thy word.

No. 66.   WILL YOU BRING THEM IN?

IDA M. BUDD.   C. D. EMERSON.

1. Far a - way up - on the mountain, With their rugged paths and steep,
2. On the de - sert bare and lone - ly, With its gleaming, scorching sands,
3. You have felt the joy of par-don, You have proved His promise true;

Wand'ring in the night and darkness, Are the Master's straying sheep,
Souls are roam-ing, faint and wea - ry, Longing for God's pasture lands;
Have you told some err - ing broth - er What the Lord has done for you?

And the Mas - ter calls for help - ers Those be-nighted souls to win;
Long-ing still, but still in bond-age To the aw - ful pow'r of sin;
Can you dare to plead *for* sin - ners If you will not *with* them plead?

Who will of - fer for the ser - vice? Who will go and bring them in?
Who will help them break their fet-ters? Who will seek to bring them in?
Will you bring them to the Sav - ior Who can make them free indeed?

CHORUS.

Will you seek............ the lost to win............ From the
the lost to win?   Will you seek the lost to win?

Will You Bring Them In?

dark - - en'd ways of sin?........... For the sake......

From the ways of sin, from the darken'd ways of sin? For the sake

of Him who saves you Will you go........ and bring them in?........

Will you go and bring them in, Will you go and bring them in.

No. 67. JESUS DIED FOR ME.

FINE.

1. { A - las! and did my Sav-ior bleed? And did my Sovereign die?
    { Would He de - vote that sa - cred head[Omit.....................]

D.C.—Yes, Je - sus died for all man-kind; Bless God, sal - va - tion's free!

CHORUS.   D. C.

For such a worm as I?   Je-sus died for you,   Je-sus died for me,

for you,   for me,

2 Was it for crimes that I have done.
  He groaned upon the tree?
Amazing pity! grace unknown!
  And love beyond degree!

3 Well might the sun in darkness hide.
  And shut his glories in,
When Christ, the mighty Maker, died
  For man, the creature's sin!

4 Thus might I hide my blushing face,
  While His dear cross appears;
Dissolve my heart in thankfulness,
  And melt mine eyes to tears.

5 But drops of grief can ne'er repay
  The debt of love I owe:
Here, Lord, I give myself away,
  'Tis all that I can do.

No. 68.　　SIMPLY TRUSTING.

D. C. CARSON.

ADOLPH JESRAEL.

1. Sim-ply by trust-ing, the Sav-ior I sought; Simply by trusting, my
2. Sim-ply by trust-ing, I walk in the light; Simply by trusting, all
3. Sim-ply I'm trust-ing, in sickness or health; Trusting in pov - er - ty,

par-don was wrought; Sim - ply by trust-ing, my doubtings all cease;
stains are made white; Trusting the Ho - ly One, kept from all sin,
trust-ing in wealth; Trusting Him whol-ly, where-e'er my lot's cast,

CHORUS.

Trusting in Je - sus I find a sweet peace. ⎫ Trust - ing,
Trusting Him ful - ly, I'm pure now with-in. ⎬
Yes, in Thee, Savior, I'll trust to the last. ⎭ Trusting in Je - sus I'm

filled with His love; Trust - ing, fed from a - bove; Trusting, I'm
filled with His love; Trusting His merits, I'm fed from a - bove.

kept by His pow'r di-vine; Trusting Thee, Savior, I know Thou art mine.

No. 69. SHINE, SHINE, SHINE!

E. A. S. H.

Eva A. S. Higgins.

1. Je - sus bids us shine with a bright, bright light! Pure lit - tle
2. Je - sus bids us fol - low, where He may lead; All that He
3. Je - sus bids us love Him with all our heart; Oh, from His

gems in the Sav - ior's sight; Shin-ing for the Mas - ter with
tells us we'll try to heed; Scat - ter - ing a - bout us the
love may we nev - er part; But, while lit - tle child - ren, for

Chorus.

all our might, Shine, shine, shine.)
gos - pel seed, Shine, shine, shine. } Bright lit - tle jew _ - els
heav'n we'll start; Shine, shine, shine.)

we will be; Shin - ing with a light that all can see;

Hear the Mas-ter's voice say-ing: "Shine for me!" Shine, shine, shine.

No. 70. JESUS IS MIGHTY TO SAVE.

Mrs. Ida M. Budd.   CHAS. H. Gabriel.

1. Thou who art lost in the maz-es of sin, Je-sus can save!
2. Pre-cious the promise to those who be-lieve, Je-sus can save!
3. Trust Him, and prove Him, and then thou shalt know Je-sus can save!

Je-sus can save! Hark! He is ten-der-ly call-ing thee in,
Je-sus can save! You may this mo-ment His cleansing re-ceive,
Je-sus can save! They who to God thro' the dear Sav-ior go,

Je-sus is might-y to save! In from the darkness to
Je-sus is will-ing to save! Come un-to Him for where
Find He is long-ing to save! Still He is call-ing; O

walk in the light; In from the dangers that lurk in the night;
else canst thou go? See! He is wait-ing His grace to be-stow;
hear Him to-day! Quench not the spir-it that bids thee o-bey;

Into the sunshine of love, warm and bright, O He is mighty to save!
Sins that are scarlet He'll wash white as snow, O He is will-ing to save!
Haste, to the fount of His mer-cy a-way, Je-sus is long-ing to save!

Jesus is Mighty to Save.

CHORUS

Je - - - sus is mighty to save, might - y   to save;
Je-sus is might-y, is might-y to save,   Je-sus is might-y, is might-y to save;

They who will trust Him shall find evermore, Je-sus is mighty to save.

No. 71.   HALLELUJAH.

ISAAC NAYLOR.

Hal - le-lu - jah! hal - le - lu - jah! hal - le - lu - jah! hal - le-lu-jah!

Hal-le - lu-jah! hal-le - lu-jah! Hal-le-lu - jah! hal-le-lu-jah! hal-le -

lu - jah, A-men, A-men, A-men, hal-le-lu-jah! ha-le-lu-jah! A - men.

No. 72. WHITER THAN SNOW.

JAMES NICHOLSON. WM. G. FISCHER.

1. Lord Je-sus, I long to be per-fect-ly whole; I want Thee for-
2. Lord Je-sus, look down from Thy throne in the skies, And help me to
3. Lord Je-sus, for this, I most hum-bly en-treat, I wait, bless-ed
4. Lord Je-sus, Thou see-st I pa-tient-ly wait,, Come now, and with-

ev-er to live in my soul, Break down ev-'ry i-dol, cast
make a com-plete sac-ri-fice; I give up my-self, and what-
Lord, at Thy cru-ci-fied feet, By faith, for my cleansing, I
in me a new heart cre-ate; To those who have sought Thee, Thou

out ev-'ry foe; Now wash me, and I shall be whit-er than snow.
ev-er I know Now wash me, and I shall be whit-er than snow.
see Thy blood flow. Now wash me, and I shall be whit-er than snow.
nev-er said'st "No," Now wash me, and I shall be whit-er than snow.

CHORUS.

Whit-er than snow, yes, whit-er than snow; Now

wash me, and I shall be whit-er than snow.

No. 73. BE A GOLDEN SUNBEAM.

Isaac Naylor.

Chas. H. Gabriel.

1. Be a gold - en sun-beam, ra - di - ant and bright, Chasing from life's
2. When the way is gloom-y, cheer it with a song,— Ban - ish mist and
3. Be a gold - en sun-beam, bright, and pure, and fair; With thy smiles and

path - way sor - row's frowning night; With thy gold - en sun - light
shad - ow as you march a - long; In the place of bri - ars,
son - nets light - en hu - man care; With the sweet-est mu - sic

dry the dew-y tear, Scat-ter from the sad heart all its doubt and fear.
strew the fairest flow'rs, Wreathing brows with roses pluck'd from heav'nly bow'rs.
from the harp of love, Lure the sad and wea - ry to our home a - bove.

CHORUS

{ Be a gold - en sun-beam, beau - ti - ful and bright, Scat-ter - ing
{ Be a gold - en sun-beam, joy - ful - ly and glad, Scat-ter - ing

clouds and darkness with thy shining light:
rays of sun-light

when the way is sad.

No. 74. I LOVE TO THINK OF JESUS.

W. A. O.
W. A. OGDEN.

1. Oh! I love to think of Je - sus by the blue, blue sea, As He
2. Oh! I love to think of Je - sus when at Sych -ar's well, And I
3. Oh! I love to think of Je - sus as He lived on earth, And I

walked up - on the shores of the roll - ing Gal - i - lee; There the
love to hear the sto - ry my Sav - ior there did tell, Of the
love to pon-der o - ver His good-ness and His worth; How to

mul - ti-tude He fed thro' a mir - a - cle in - deed, And He
wa - ter He would give, say -ing "they who drink shall live!" And shall
sin-ners He was kind, how He healed the sick and blind, Ev - en

CHORUS.

bade the fish-ers "Fol-low me!" Won - der-ful the love......
nev - er, nev - er thirst a-gain.
called the dead to life a-gain. Wonderful the love, O wonderful the love

1 That brought my Sav - ior down,......... 2 wrought for me a crown.
That brought my Savior down, That brought my Savior down;

No. 75. TRUST IN THE LORD.

ADA BLENKHORN. CHAS. H. GABRIEL.

1. Go forth in the name of your conquering Lord, Pro-tec-tion and
2. Tho' fierce the temptations your soul that as-sail, Tho' keen is the
3. Be strong in the Lord, in the strength of His might! Before you, in

help He will dai-ly af-ford; Go trust-ing the promise of
con-flict, it shall not pre-vail; Be brave and courageous where-
haste, all your foes shall take flight; And when you are called o-ver

grace to sus-tain; He'll give you the vic-t'ry a-gain and a-gain.
ev-er you go, In Christ you shall triumph against ev-'ry foe.
Jor-dan's dark tide, You'll shout hal-le-lu-jah with Christ at your side.

CHORUS.

Trust in the Lord, He is mighty to save you! Trust in the Sav-ior, and be not dismayed!

Tho' storms rage around you, His love will a-bide, And in His pa-vil-ion you safely may hide.

No. 76. THE STRANGER AT THE DOOR.

T. C. O'KANE.

1. Be-hold a stran-ger at the door; He gently knocks–has knocked be-fore;
2. O love - ly at - ti-tude–He stands With melting heart and pierced hands;
3. But will He prove a friend in-deed? He will—the ver-y friend you need;
4. Rise, touch'd with grat-i-tude divine : Turn out His en - e - my and thine:
5. Ad-mit Him, ere His an-ger burn–His feet, de-part-ed, ne'er re-turn;

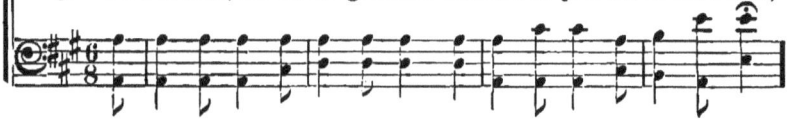

Has wait-ed long, is wait-ing still : You treat no oth - er friend so ill.
O matchless kindness–and He shows This matchless kindness to His foes.
The friend of sin-ners? Yes, 'tis He, With garments dyed on Cal-va-ry.
That soul-de-stroy-ing monster–sin, And let the Heav'nly Stranger in.
Ad-mit Him, or the hour's at hand, You'll at *His* door re-ject-ed stand.

REFRAIN.

O, let the dear Sav-ior come in, He'll cleanse the heart from sin;
come in, from sin;

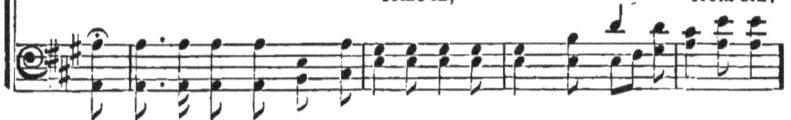

O, keep Him no more out at the door, But let the dear Savior come in.
come in.

No. 77.   WORK FOR JESUS.

JAMES ROWE.   COPYRIGHT, 1900, BY CHAS. H. GABRIEL.   W. E. M. HACKLEMAN, OWNER.   ORAN WILLIAMS.

May be sung in D♭.

1. In this vale of sadness, Grief, and pain, and care, Where the burdened
2. Ever hearts are breaking; Cries are ev - er heard; Ev - er struggling
3. There are souls around you, Deep in doubt and sin, Whom an act of

and the wea - ry Meet you ev - 'ry - where; Oh, what precious blessings
souls are long-ing For a cheer-ing word; Oh, what deeds of kindness
love might rescue, Whom a word might win; Oh, what err-ing brothers

D. S.—Oh, what precious blessings

FINE.

May be yours each day, If you'll work for Je-sus All a-long the way.
You may do each day, If you'll work for Je-sus All a-long the way.
You may win each day, If you'll work for Je-sus All a-long the way.

May be yours each day,   If you'll work for Jesus All a-long the way.

CHORUS.

Work   for   Je - sus,   Help the dear Re-deem - er,
Work for Je - sus, work for Je - sus,

D.S.

Soothe   and   com - fort,   Gladden while you may;....
Soothe and com - fort, soothe and com - fort, Glad - den   while you may;

No. 78. LIVING, WALKING, WORKING.

N. A. McA.

Rev. N. A. McAULAY.

1. I am liv-ing in the sun-shine Of my Sav ior's precious love;
2. I am walking in the pre-cepts Of my Sav-ior's ho-ly word;
3. I am working in the vine-yard For my Mas-ter ev-'ry day;

I have felt his rays of glo-ry Shin-ing from the throne a-bove.
I en-joy the sweetest rapt-ure, In com-mun-ion with my Lord.
I am pointing need-y sin-ners To the new and liv-ing Way.

I am trust-ing in the mer-cy That redeemed my soul from sin;
I am sing-ing Je-sus' prais-es, For His spir-it gives me joy;
I am tell-ing forth the sto-ry Of the Lamb for sin-ners slain;

I have felt the ho-ly cleansing That has made me pure with-in.
He has filled my soul with gladness That the world can-not de-stroy.
I will toil till life is end-ed, And I go, with Christ to reign.

No. 79. VICTORY IS COMING.

ALIDA ROE. J. S. FEARIS.

1. Vic - to-ry is com-ing! Send the word a-long. Let the glo-rious
2. See our host advancing! hear our hap-py song; See our shields of
3. Vic - to-ry is com-ing! peace will fol-low soon, Bring-ing joy e -

ban-ner wave on high! Sa-tan's hosts are trembling.Right must vanquish wrong,
faith all gleaming bright! New re-cruits are joining as we march a-long,
ter-nal in its smile; What a vast array will stand before the throne,

CHORUS.

Vic-tor - y is com-ing by and bye!)
Leav-ing all to bat-tle for the right. } Join,ye Christian warriors, in a
When the cap-tives join our rank and file.)

glad triumphant song! Let the nations hear us as we march a-long! Nev-er rest nor

falter, banish sin and wrong; Victory is coming by and bye!
by and bye!

No. 80.   "SINCE I HAVE OVERCOME."

QUARTET.

IDA M. BUDD,   CHAS. H. GABRIEL.

1. Sad hearts for-get your doubts and fears, Nor vexed and troubled be;
2. My Fa-ther's house hath mansions fair For all who do His will:

As in the Fa-ther ye be-lieve, Oh, trust ye thus in me;
I go your dwelling to pre-pare, My prom - ise to ful - fill;

Yea, trust in me, with Christ the Lord, Nor heed earth's warring strife—
"I am the way, the truth, the life, Come, then, and learn of me,

"He that be - liev - eth on the Son, Hath ev - er - last-ing life."
That where I am for ev - er - more There ye may al - so be."

REFRAIN.
Sop. and Alto.

"Al - tho' the world hath woe and pain For those who seek that home,

"Since I Have Overcome."

Tenor and Alto.

Yet, ye shall more than conq'rors be, Since I have o - ver-come,

Yet, ye shall more than conq'rors be, Since I have o - ver-come."

"Since I have o - ver-come."

No. 81.   YE CHRISTIAN HERALDS.

1. Ye Chris - tian her - alds, go, pro - claim Sal -
2. He'll shield you with a wall of fire, With
3. And when our la - bors all are o'er, Then

va - tion thro' Im - man - uel's name; To dis - tant climes
flam - ing zeal your hearts in - spire, Bid ra - ging winds
we shall meet to part no more—Meet with the blood-

the ti - dings bear, And plant the Rose of Shar - on there.
their fu - ry cease, And hush the temp-est in - to peace.
bought throng to fall, And crown our Je - sus Lord of all.

No. 82. ETERNAL GOODNESS.

JOHN G. WHITTIER. ORAN WILLIAMS.

1. I know not what the future hath Of mar-vel or sur-prise,
2. And if my heart and flesh are weak To bear an un-tried pain,
3. I know not where His is-lands lift Their fronded palms in air;

As-sured a - lone that life and death His mer-cy un - der - lies.
The bruis - ed reed He will not break, But strengthen and sus-tain.
I on - ly know I can not drift Be-yond His love and care.

CHORUS.

And so be - side........... the Si - lent Sea,...........
And so be - side the Si - lent Sea,

I, trust - ing, wait........... the muf-fled oar;..........
I, trust-ing, wait, I wait the muf-fled oar;

No harm from Him........... can come to me,...........
No harm from Him can come to me,

Eternal Goodness.

Up - on the o - cean or on shore............
Up - on the o - cean or up - on the shore.

No. 83. PASS ME NOT.

FANNY J. CROSBY. W. H. DOANE.

1. Pass me not, O gen-tle Sav - ior, Hear my hum-ble cry;
2. Let me, at Thy throne of mer - cy Find a sweet re - lief;
3. Trust-ing on - ly in Thy mer - its, Would I seek Thy face;
4. Thou, the spring of all my com - fort, More than life to me—

FINE.

While on oth - ers Thou art smil - ing, Do not pass me by.
Kneel - ing there in deep con - tri - tion, Help my un - be - lief.
Heal my wounded, bro - ken spir - it, Save me by Thy grace.
Whom have I on earth be - side Thee? Whom in heav'n but Thee?

D. S.—*While on oth - ers Thou art call - ing, Do not pass me by.*

REFRAIN. D. S.

Sav - ior, - Sav ior, Hear my hum - ble cry;

No. 84. OUR WATCHWORD.

SILAS FARMER. CHAS. H. GABRIEL.

1. We're draw-ing near to Je - sus, Our ban - ner waves on high;
2. We love our Mas - ter's serv - ice, And, see - ing eye to eye,
3. The fields are white to har - vest, The days are speed - ing by;

And this our watch-word ev - er, "We'll work un - til we die."
With grace di - vine to help us, We'll work un - til we die.
Go forth a - gain, ye work - ers, And work un - til ye die.

CHORUS.

We'll work.............. un - til we die;.............. The
work un - til we die, Yes, we'll work un - til we die;

ban - ner of our Cap-tain through the con - flict we will bear; We'll

work...... un-til we die........ And then go home our crowns to wear.
work until we die, yes, we'll work until we die,

No. 85. SOME DAY.

BY PER. OF J. J. HOOD, OWNER OF COPYRIGHT.

EBEN E. REXFORD.   FRANK M. DAVIS.

DUET.

1. I hear a song, a song so sweet, I try all vain - ly to re - peat;
2. Some day my journey will be done, Earth will be lost and heaven won;
3. Some day I say, content to wait The opening of the jas-per gate;
4. When comes the time for me to go, The homeward path I may not know;

Cres.

Its mel - o - dy and feeling say, I'll sing it if God wills some day.
And when the long rough way is trod, I shall be - hold the face of God.
Come soon or late, that day will be The dawn of end - less rest for me.
But in God's hand my own I'll lay, And He will lead me home some day.

CHORUS.

Some day, some hap - py day to be, My voice will learn its mel-o-
Some hap-py day, a day to be, My voice will learn its

Cres. *Rit.*

dy, And I shall sing the songs so sweet, Of rest and heav'n, at Jesus' feet.
mel - o - dy,

No. 86. LOOKING UNTO JESUS.

Rev. N. A. McAulay. CHAS. H. Gabriel.

Tenor or Soprano and Alto.

1. Look - ing un - to Je - sus as I run the christian race;
2. Look - ing un - to Je - sus when I feel the sting of sin;
3. Look - ing un - to Je - sus, singing sweet - ly as I go;

Look - ing un - to Je - sus for sup-plies of dai - ly grace;
Look - ing un - to Je - sus for His cleans-ing pow'r with-in;
Look - ing un - to Je - sus till I quit this vale be - low;

Look - ing un - to Je - sus as I read His ho - ly word;
Look - ing un - to Je - sus for a peace with-out al - loy
Look - ing un - to Je - sus when im -mor - tal I shall rise,

Look - ing un - to Je - sus, my Re-deem - er and my Lord.
Look - ing un - to Je - sus for a nev - er end-ing joy.
Look - ing un - to Je - sus for a home be-yond the skies.

CHORUS.

Look - - - ing un - to Je - sus, Look - - - ing ev - 'ry
Looking, look - ing, look-ing un - to Je-sus, Look-ing, look - ing,

Looking Unto Jesus. Concluded.

day; Look - ing un - to Je - sus, To
look-ing ev -'ry day; Looking,look - ing, look- ing un - to Je - sus,

Him who is the way.......... Look-ing un - to Je - sus in the
Looking un - to Him, to Him who is the way.

conflict and the strife, Looking unto Je -sus ev'ry mo- ment of my life.
Je - sus ev'ry moment of my life.

If desired, this ending may be sung as a Duet.

No. 87. WELLESLEY.

F. W. FABER. LIZZIE S. TOURJEE.

1. There's a wide-ness in God's mer- cy, Like the wide-ness of the sea;
2. There's a wel-come for the sin. - ner, And more grac-es for the good;
3. For the love of God is broad- er Than the meas-ure of man's mind;
4. If our love were but more sim-ple, We should take Him at His word;

There's a kind -ness in His jus - tice. Which is more than lib - er - ty.
There is mer - cy with the Sav - ior; There is heal-ing in His blood.
And the heart of the E - ter - nal Is most won-der-ful - ly kind.
And our lives would be all sun-shine In the sweetness of our Lord.

No. 88. HERE AM I.

ADA BLENKHORN. Dr. S. B. JACKSON.

1. When the morning sun is bright, And the harvest fields are white, And the
2. There are famished souls to feed, There are wand'ring steps to lead; From the
3. There are bat-tles yet to win, 'Gainst the marshalled host of sin, And the

ones that should be reaping In the fields, are loit'ring by; When the
depths of sin and darkness, There are helpless ones that cry: "Who will
Sav-ior, in each con-flict Swift to help, is ev-er nigh; When He

Mas-ter's voice is ring-ing O'er the fields of wav-ing grain,
feed 'the hun-gry chil-dren, Who will seek the lost to save?"
calls for deeds of dar-ing, And for loy-al hearts and true,

D. S.—*ev - er Thou wilt have me do to glo - ri - fy Thy name,*
FINE.

Call - ing loud for reap-ers! an-swer, "Here am I, Here am I!"
Je - sus calls you, who will an-swer, "Here am I, Here am I!"
Read-y will I be to an-swer, "Here am I, Here am I!"

Speak, O Lord, Thy servant hear-eth, Here am I, Here am I!"

CHORUS.

When I hear . . . . . . the voice of my Sav - - ior.
When I hear the lov - ing voice, the lov - ing voice of my Sav-ior,

Here Am I.

D. S.

I will quickly, gladly give to Him the re-ply, "What-so-
the glad re-ply,

No. 89.   BLESS THE LORD.

COPYRIGHT, 1897, BY W. E. M. HACKLEMAN.

J. V. C.

J. V. COOMBS.

DUET. SOPRANO and TENOR.

1. Dear - est Lord, hear our prayer; Keep us close to Thy side;
2. Fill our hearts with Thy love; To the cross help us cling;
3. Change our tears in - to joy; Bless us, Lord, on this day;

Be our Friend and Pro - tect - or, Our Sav - ior and Guide.
And we'll praise Thee for - ev - er, Lord Je - sus, our King.
Teach - ing us how to wor - ship, To sing, and to pray.

CHORUS.

Bless the Lord, praise His name; Bless the Lord, praise His
Bless the Lord, praise His name; Bless the Lord,

name; Bless the Lord, O my soul, Bless the Lord, O my soul.
praise His name;

HAPPY VOICES.

J. M. DUNGAN.

1. Singing in the ear - ly morn - ing, Singing all the sun-ny day,
2. List then to the hap - py voi - ces Tell-ing of the Savior's love;
3. So we'll bless the lit - tle chil - dren For their songs of joy and love,

Hear the children's voices sing - ing, Cheering us a-long the way;
Sing-ing o'er and o'er the sto - ry Of the blessed home a - bove,
That will lead us ev - er near - er To our heav'nly home a - bove;

Where sometimes the path is thorn - y, And the way is dark and drear,
Where at last we'll meet the loved ones Who have reached the oth-er shore,
Let us make their pathway bright-er, Let us ev-'ry kind-ness show,

Then the simple faith of childhood Will drive away each doubt and fear.
And are calling us to fol - low Where we'll sorrow nev-er more.
For Christ loved the lit - tle chil - dren, When in this world of sin and woe.

CHORUS.

Sing - ing all the way, Mer - ry ev'ry day;
Singing all the way, yes, singing all the way, Merry ev'ry day, yes, merry ev'ry day;

Happy Voices.

List......we to their happy voices Sing - ing all the way.
List we to their voices, to their happy voices, Singing all the way, yes, singing all the way.

No. 91.   OH, HOW I LOVE JESUS.

ISAAC WATTS.

1. A - las! and did my Sav - ior bleed? And did my Sov'reign die?
2. Was it for crimes that I had done, He groaned up-on the tree?
3. Well might the sun in dark-ness hide, And shut his glo - ries in,
4. Thus might I hide my blush-ing face While His dear cross ap - pears;
5. But drops of grief can ne'er re-pay The debt of love I owe;

FINE.

Would He de-vote that sa - cred head For such a worm as I?
A - maz - ing pit - y! grace unknown! And love be-yond de - gree!
When God's own Son was cru - ci - fied For man, the creature's sin.
Dis solve my heart in thank-ful-ness, And melt mine eyes to tears.
Here, Lord, I give my-self a-way—'Tis all that I can do.

D. S.—Oh, how I love Je - sus, Be-cause He first loved me.

CHORUS.   D. S.

Oh, how I love Je - sus, Oh, how I love Je - sus,

No. 92. THE MASTER IS CALLING.

Mrs. HARRIET E. JONES.   CHAS. H. GABRIEL.

1. My broth-er, the Mas-ter is call-ing for thee, Call-ing for
2. The Mas-ter is call-ing, O make Him your choice; Call-ing for
3. The Mas-ter-is call-ing, the Mas-ter who gave—Call-ing for

thee, He is call-ing for thee; The full-ness of rich-es He of-fers you
thee, He is call-ing for thee; If you will accept Him, yonr soul will re
thee, He is call-ing for thee; His life for the sin-ner, the might-y to-

free,—He's call-ing for thee, for thee; He lov-ing-ly, ten-der-ly
joice,—He's call-ing for thee, for thee; He's wait-ing so pa-tient-ly
save,—He's call-ing for thee, for thee; Ac-cept Him, my broth-er, get

calls you to-day, O will you ac-cept Him? how can you de-lay!
now to re-ceive; O fly to Him, brother, look up and be-lieve.
un-der the blood, Be white as the snow thro' the soul-cleansing flood.

CHORUS.

Call - - ing for thee,   He's call - - ing for
Call-ing for thee,   He's call-ing for thee, the Mas-ter is call-ing, is

The Master is Calling.

thee! . . . O haste to His feet and in pen-i-tence bow, For He's
call - ing for thee!

call - - - ing now; . . Call - - ing for
call - ing He's call - ing thee now, just now; Call - ing for thee, He is

thee, ... He is call - - ing for thee . . . . So
call - ing for thee, The Mas - ter is call - ing, is call-ing for thee, So

lov - ing-ly, ten - der-ly call - - ing for thee . . . . . .
lov - ing-ly, ten - der - ly call - ing, He's call-ing for thee, for thee.

No. 93. MY FAITH LOOKS UP TO THEE.

1 My faith looks up to Thee,
  Thou Lamb of Calvary,
    Savior divine;
  Now hear me while I pray:
  Take all my guilt away;
  O let me from this day
    Be wholly thine.

2 May Thy rich grace impart
  Strength to my fainting heart;
    My zeal inspire;

As Thou hast died for me,
O may my love to Thee
Pure, warm and changeless be,
  A living fire.

3 While life's dark maze I tread,
  And griefs around me spread,
    Be Thou my guide;
  Bid darkness turn to day;
  Wipe sorrow's tears away,
  Nor let me ever stray
    From Thee away.

No. 94. GLORIOUS NEWS.

E. E. HEWITT.　　　　　　　　　　　　　　　CHAS. H. GABRIEL.

1. Car-ry the message to lands far a-way, Glorious news! glorious news!
2. We have a Sav-ior with mer-cy for all, Glorious news! glorious news!
3. Je-sus will use us in spreading His word, Glorious news! glorious news!

We have a Sav-ior who's liv-ing to-day, Glorious, glorious news!
Wide as the world is His free lov-ing call, Glorious, glorious news!
Not un-to an-gels this hon-or conferred, Glorious, glorious news!

Liv-ing to save who-so-ev-er will come, Liv-ing to welcome the
Let all who hear send the message a-long, Till oth-er voic-es shall
We who have plung'd in the fountain of love, O-pened our hearts to the

wan-der-er home; Send the glad word ring-ing o-ver the foam,
join in the song, Swell-ing the praise of the glo-ri-fied throng,
Heav-en-ly Dove, We can win jew-els for man-sions a-bove,

CHORUS.

Glo-rious, glo-rious news! Tell the glad news, glo-rious news,
the glo-rious news,

Glorious News.

Car - ry the mes-sage to lands far a - way! Tell the glad news, the glo - rious news, We have a Sav - ior who's liv - ing to - day.

glo - rious news,

No . 95. BATTLE HYMN OF MISSIONS.

RAY PALMER.　　　　　　　　　　　　JOHN WHITAKER.

1. E - ter - nal Fa - ther, Thou hast said, That Christ all
2. We wait Thy tri - umph, Sav - ior, King; Long a - ges
3. Thy hosts are mus-tered to the field; "The Cross! the

glo - ry shall ob - tain; That He who once a suf - f'rer
have pre - pared Thy way; Now all a - broad thy ban - ner
Cross!" the bat - tle call; The old grim tow'rs of dark-ness

No. 96.   THE ARMIES OF GOD.

C. D. EMERSON.   W. E. M. HACKLEMAN, OWNER.   GEO. C. HUGG.

1. { O Chris-tian, gird the ar - mor on, And press the fight with sin! }
{ Go forth a- gainst the hosts of wrong, Go forth our cause to win; }

2. { O Chris-tian, gird the ar - mor on, And has - ten to the field; }
{ A-gainst the powr's of darkness go, De - ter-mined not to yield! }

3. { O Chris-tian, gird the ar - mor on, The world is watch-ing thee; }
{ With pray'r and suppli-ca - tion press A - long to vic - to - ry! }

The con-flict wild-ly ra - ges, No long - er then de - lay,
Clad in a full sal - va - tion, The Spir - it's sword in hand,
Be loy - al to His serv - ice, His truth to all pro-claim;

But, trust-ing in Je - ho-vah's might. Go! watch, and fight, and pray.
From vic-t'ry un - to vic - t'ry go! It is the Lord's command.
God loves a val-iant war - ri - or, Then go in Je - sus' name.

CHORUS.

Hal-le - lu - jah! they are marching on, Hal-le-lu - jah! praise the
Hal-le-lu- jah!   Hal-le-lu - jah!

Lord! The ar-mies of the liv - ing God are march - ing on.
praise the Lord!   marching, marching on.

No. 97.   MORE PRECIOUS EVERY DAY.

Rev. W. C. Martin.

Chas. H. Gabriel.

1. How deep is that great love which all The wounds of Jesus Christ dis-play;
2. The sun has dawn'd up-on my soul With beaming, pure, life-giv-ing ray;
3. He com-forts me in sad-dest mood. He seeks me when I go a-stray;
4. In dark-ness Je - sus is my light, My sure de-fence, my help, my stay;

'Twas sweet when first I heard His call, And grows more precious ev-'ry day.
I love His gen-tle, sweet con-trol—He grows more precious ev-'ry day.
My wild-est pas-sions are subdued, He grows more precious ev-'ry day.
My cour-age in the darkest night—He grows more precious ev-'ry day.

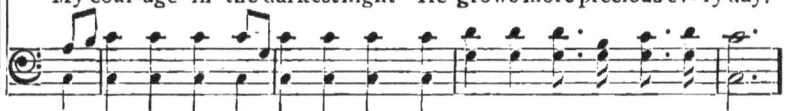

CHORUS.

Ev -'ry day,.......... ev -'ry day,.......... At His word the
Ev -'ry day, ev -'ry day, At His word of

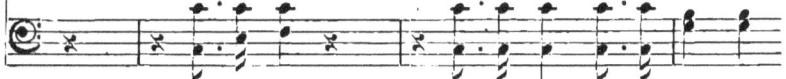

shad - ows backward roll;.............. Ev -'ry day...........
love the shad - ows back-ward roll; Ev -'ry day

a-long the way........... Je - sus grows more precious to my soul.
a - long the way

No. 98. I'LL GO WITH HIM.

JENNIE REE.　　　　　　　　　　　　　CHAS. H. GABRIEL.

1. He will hide me in His pa-vil-ion, He will shield me from the foe,
2. "He will cov-er me with His feathers," Me from famine He will keep;
3. He will guide me to fields e-ter-nal, When the day of life is past;

He will lead me in pastures ver-nal, Where the cool-ing wa-ters flow.
He, the Shepherd, will not for-sake me, Tho' a wayward, wand'ring sheep.
Thro' the val-ley of shad-ows safe-ly He will lead me home at last.

CHORUS.

I'll go with Him, I'll go with Him, Lead me,
I'll go with Him, I'll go with Him,

Lord, I'll fol-low Thee; I'll go with Him,
Lead me, Lord, I'll fol-low, fol-low Thee; I'll go with Him,

I'll go with Him, Lead me, Lord, I'll fol-low Thee.
I'll go with Him, Lead me, Lord, I'll fol-low, fol-low Thee.

No. 99.   MY STRENGTH AND STAY.

JOHN G. WHITTIER.   ORAN WILLIAMS.

1. When on my day of life the night is fall - ing, And, in the winds
2.   I have but Thee, my Father! let Thy spir-it   Be with me then
3. Some humble door a - mong Thy many mansions, Some shelt'ring shade
4. There, from the mu-sic round a-bout me steal-ing,   I fain would learn

from un-seen spaces blown, Voices   I hear from out the darkness call-
to comfort and up-hold ; No gate of pearl, no branch of palm I mer-
where sin and striving cease, And flows for-ev -er thro' the green ex-pan-
the new and ho - ly song, And find at last, beneath Thy trees of heal-

D. S.—*Help-er, ev - er pres-*

FINE.   **CHORUS.**

ing My feet to paths unknown:
it, Nor street of shining gold.   Be   Thou my strength,
sions, The riv- er of Thy peace.
ing, The life for which I long.   Be Thou my strength, Be Thou my stay,

ent, Be Thou my strength and stay.

D. S.

Be   Thou my stay,   O Love di - vine, O
Be Thou my strength,   Be Thou my stay.

No. 100. COME TO THE FEAST.

CHARLOTTE G. HOMER.　　　　　　　　　　　　　W. A. OGDEN.

1. "All things are ready," come to the feast! Come, for the ta - ble now is
2. "All things are ready," come to the feast! Come, for the door is o - pen
3. "All things are ready," come to the feast! Come, while He waits to welcome
4. "All things are ready," come to the feast! Leave ev-'ry care and worldly

spread; Ye fam-ish-ing, ye weary, come, And thou shalt be richly fed.
wide; A place of hon - or is reserv'd For you at the Master's side.
thee; De-lay not while this day is thine, To-mor-row may nev-er be.
strife; Come, feast upon the love of God, And drink ev-er-last-ing life.

CHORUS.

Hear . . . . the in - vi - ta - tion, Come, "who - - so - ev - er
Hear the in - vi-ta - tion, "Who-so-ev-er will," Hear the in-vi - ta - tion,

will;" . . . . Praise God . . . . for full sal-
"Who - so - ev - er will;" Praise God for full sal - va - tion For

va - - - tion For "who - so - ev - er - will."
"who - so - ev - er will.",

No. 101.　BLESSED ASSURANCE.

FANNIE CROSBY.

Mrs. J. F. KNAPP.

1. Bless - ed as - sur - ance, Je - sus is mine! Oh, what a
2. Per - fect sub - mis - sion, per - fect de - light, Vis - ions of
3. Per - fect sub - mis - sion, all is at rest, I in my

fore-taste of glo - ry di - vine! Heir of sal - va - tion, pur-chase of
rap - ture now burst on my sight, An - gels de-scend-ing, bring from a-
Sav - ior am hap - py and blest, Watching and wait-ing, look - ing a-

CHORUS.

God, Born of His spir - it, washed in His blood. This is my sto - ry,
bove, Ech - oes of mer - cy, whis-pers of love.
bove, Filled with His goodness, lost in His love.

this is my song, Praising my Sav-ior all the day long; This is my

sto - ry, this is my song, Praising my Sav-ior all the day long.

No. 102. SUNSHINE IN THE HOME.

HELEN L. DUNGAN.

J. M. DUNGAN.

1. We can make the whole day brighter By some kind, un-self-ish deed,
2. Lit - tle words so full of mean - ing, Kind-ly spo - ken by the way,
3. Let the home that God has giv - en, In His kind-uess full and free,

Make the heav - y bur-den light - er, Help our dear ones in their need;
Will be treas-ures for the glean - ing At the close of life's brief day;
Be a type of that in heav - en, Where we'll rest e - ter - nal - ly;

For the time grows nearer, near - er When they'll pass from us a - way;
For there comes a time of reap - ing. When we gath - er gold en grain,
May its light thro' darkness streaming. Showing forth the Savior's love,

And their loving hearts grow dear-er As they near the per-fect day.
When with joy, in-stead of weep-ing, We will meet our loved a - gain.
Lead some lost one by its beam-ing To the bless-ed home a - bove.

CHORUS.

Scatter the sunshine in the home to-day, Scatter the sunshine, scatter the sunshine,
in the home to-day,

Sunshine In the Home.

It will bring joy and blessing all the way, Scatter the sunshine in the home.

the home.

No. 103. PRAISE THE NAME OF JESUS.

COPYRIGHT, 1902, BY W. E. M HACKLEMAN.

HELEN L. DUNGAN.   J. M. DUNGAN.

1. Praise the name of Jesus for His tender care, Watch-ing o'er me ev - 'ry day;
2. For my Sav-ior is my never-failing Friend Thro' the night and thro' the day;
3. Tho' the dark'ning shadows round about me creep, And the way is lone and drear,

He will bear my burdens, hear my feeble prayer, And will guide me when I stray.
On His love I know I always can depend, So I'll praise Him ev'ry day.
By my Savior's side I'll ever closely keep, Singing happy songs of cheer.

CHORUS.

All the way,   all the way,   I will praise His name ev'ry day,
All the way,   all the way,

I am happy in my blessed Savior's love, And I'm singing all the way.

No. 104. ARE WE WILLING?

IDA M. BUDD.   ORAM WILLIAMS.

1. Are we will-ing to walk with Je - sus, By faith as well as by
2. Are we will-ing to speak for Je - sus, To tell the ran-som He
3. Are we will-ing to toil for Je - sus, Tho' oth-ers i - dly re-
4. Are we will-ing to fail for Je - sus, To bear the sting of de-

sight? Are we will - ing to fol - low His lead - ing In
gave?. And how He, in His in - fin - ite mer - cy Can
cline? In the midst of the world's liv - ing pleas-ures To
feat While the songs of the glad ones a-round us Are

dark-ness as well as in light? Can we trust to the long night
un - to the ut - ter-most save? Will we go to the lost and
serve Him thro' shadow and shine? Can we stand in the fire of
ring-ing with vic - to - ry sweet? Grant us, Sav - ior, a meek sub-

watch - es, As we trust thro' the bright glad day? And be-
wretch - ed With His mes-sage of hope and love? Will we
bat - tle With His faith as our shield well tried? Can we
mis - sion, That our will as Thine own may be; That our

Are We Willing?

lieve, tho' we can-not see Him, That He will di-rect our way?
point the sad souls and wea-ry, To mansions of rest a-bove?
rest on His gra-cious promise 'Tho' all shall be lost be-side?
hearts may be strong to la-bor, Or suf-fer or fail for Thee.

CHORUS.

O Je-sus, Thou merciful Sav-ior! A-bide in our hearts we pray,
we pray,

Rit.

And what ev-er shall be Thy bidding, May we joyfully haste to o-bey.

No. 105. MY HEAVENLY HOME.

I. { My heav'nly home is bright and fair; No pain, nor death can enter there: }
   { Its glitt'ring tow'rs the sun outshine; That heav'nly mansion shall be mine. }

CHO { I'm go-ing home, I'm go-ing home, I'm go-ing home to die no more! }
    { To die no more, to die no more; I'm go-ing home to die no more! }

2 My Father's house is built on high,
Far, far above the starry sky:
When from this earthly prison free,
That heav'nly mansion mine shall be.

3 Let others seek a home below, [flow,
Which flames devour, or waves o'er-
Be mine a happier lot to own
A heav'nly mansion near the throne.

No. 106. WHEN THE ROLL IS CALLED UP YONDER.

B. M. J.

J. M. BLACK.

1. When the trum-pet of the Lord shall sound, and time shall be no
2. On that bright and cloud-less morn-ing when the dead in Christ shall
3. Let us la-bor for the Mas-ter from the dawn till set-ting

more, And the morning breaks, e-ter-nal, bright and fair; When the
rise, And the glo-ry of His res-ur-rec-tion share; When His
sun, Let us talk of all His wondrous love and care; Then when

saved of earth shall gath-er o-ver on the oth-er shore, And the
chos-en ones shall gath-er to their home be-yond the skies, And the
all of life is o-ver, and our work on earth is done, And the

CHORUS.

roll is called up yon-der, I'll be there. When the roll....... is
roll is called up you-der, I'll be there.   When the roll is
roll is called up yon-der, we'll be there.

called up yon - - der, When the roll....... is called up
called up yon-der, I'll be there,   When the roll is called up

When the Roll Is Called up Yonder

Yon - - - der, When the roll . . . . . . is called up
Yon - der, I'll be there, When the roll is called up

yon - der, When the roll is called up yon - der, I'll be there.

No. 107. JESUS, THE CHILDREN'S FRIEND.

J. H. R. JAS. H. ROBINSON.

1. We love to sing of Je - sus, Our Savior kind and true, Because He
2. We love to work for Je - sus, And trust Him day by day, For He is
3. We love to think of Je - sus, The children's dearest Friend; And if we

REFRAIN.

loves the chil-dren, And we will love Him, too. And we will love Him, too;
ev - er read - y To help us on our way.
on-ly trust Him, He'll keep us to the end.

Yes, we will love Him too; He loves the lit-tle chil-dren, And we will love Him, too.

No. 108. FORWARD GO.

IDA M. BUDD.   C. D. EMERSON.

1. For-ward, Chris-tian sol - dier true
2. To the con - flict and the strife
3. Whereso - e'er your Lord may lead,

For - ward go!
For-ward go, for-ward go!

Hark! the Mas - ter calls for you,
Vict - 'ry means e - ter - nal life,
Nev - er vain ex - cus - es plead,

For - ward go!
Forward, for-ward, bravely go!

Put His trus-ty ar-mor on; Venture in His strength alone; Vict-'ry sure-ly
Tho' sin's host about you close, All your danger Jesus knows, He is stronger
He will your de-liv'rer be, He will make your foes to flee; His salvation

D. S. Lo! your Savior still is near! Dear His words of hope and cheer:—"I am with you

FINE. CHORUS.

will be won,
than your foes,
you shall see,
nev - er fear!"

For - ward go! For-ward go
Forward, forward glad-ly go! For-ward bravely, boldly go,

D. S.

Sounding still the battle cry! For-ward go, Resting by and by.
Forward nobly, gladly go.

No. 109. WHERE HE LEADS I'LL FOLLOW.

W. A. O.

W. A. OGDEN.

1. Sweet are the prom-is - es, Kind is the word, Dear-er far than
2. Sweet is the ten-der love Je - sus hath shown, Sweet-er far than
3. List to His lov -ing words, "Come un-to me," Wea - ry, heav - y

an - y mes-sage man ev - er heard; Pure was the mind of Christ,
an - y love that mor-tals have known; Kind to the err-ing one,
lad -en, there is sweet rest for thee; Trust in His prom-is - es,

Sin-less I see; He the great ex-am - ple is, and pat-tern for me.
Faith-ful is He: He the great ex-am - ple is, and pat-tern for me.
Faith-ful and sure; Lean up-on the Sav-ior, and thy soul is se-cure.

CHORUS.

Where............ He leads I'll fol - - low,
Where He leads I'll fol - low,
Where He leads I'll fol-low,

1

Fol - low all the way,
Fol-low all the way, yes, fol-low all the way.

2

Fol-low Je-sus ev'ry day.

No. 110. THE CHRIST WHO DIED FOR ME.

FRED WOODROW.   COPYRIGHT, 1902, BY W. E. M. HACKLEMAN.   CHAS H. GABRIEL.

SOLO, SOP. OR DUET FOR SOP. AND TENOR.

1. My heart was sore with sin and care, and dark my life with shame, Till
2. My lot was hard, my sor-rows sore, and life was dark and dim, Till
3. My feet were drawing near the grave, where none with me could go, But
4. And when up-on the shin-ing shore I find e-ter-nal peace, And

'mid the gloom I saw the light, and heard the Sav-ior's name; My
He was found to wipe my eyes, and find my rest in Him; My
o'er the Jor-dan came a hand to guide me safe-ly thro'; My
I am gathered safe-ly home where sins and sor-rows cease, I'll

load was gone, my heart was light, from bondage I was free, And
hope re-vived, my soul re-joiced, from troub-le I was free, And
tears were gone, my doubt dispelled, from ter-ror I was free, And
hear the voice and see the face of Him who set me free, And

all of it I owe to Him, the Christ who died for me.
all of it I owe to Him, the Christ who died for me.
all of it I owe to Him, the Christ who died for me.
all my joy be found in Him, the Christ who died for me.

The Christ Who Died for Me.

REFRAIN.

The Christ who died,......... who died for me, ...The Christ who
The Christ who died,

Ad lib. .... *A tempo.*

died,........who died for me,....... And all of it...........
The Christ who died, And all of it

I owe to Him,........ the Christ who died.... for me.

No. 111.   I WOULD BE THINE.*

1 I would be Thine: O take my heart and fill it with Thy love;
Thy sacred image, Lord, impart, and seal it from above.
I would be Thine: but while I strive to give myself away,
I feel rebellion still alive, and wander while I pray.

REFRAIN.—I would be Thine (I would be Thine): O take my heart
And fill it with (and fill it with) Thy tender love;
Thy sacred image, Lord, impart,
And seal it from above.

2 I would be Thine: but, Lord, I feel that evil lurks within;
Do Thou Thy majesty reveal, and banish all my sin.
I would be Thine: I would embrace the Savior, and adore;
Inspire with faith, infuse Thy grace, and now my soul restore.

—ANDREW REED.

* May be sung to the above music.

No. 112. WALKING IN THE KING'S HIGHWAY.

Mrs. Grace Weiser Davis. Chas. H. Gabriel.

1. I am hap - py ev - 'ry day, I am hap - py all the way,
2. Li - ons oft seem in the way—Straight a-head I keep, and pray,
3. I re - joice e'en when I'm sad, For His promise makes me glad,
4. Such bap - tisms of His love! Such a-noint-ings from a - bove,

Since I'm walking in the King's highway; Things may seem all right or wrong,—
Since I'm walking in the King's highway; Then a vic - to - ry is gained,
Since I m walking in the King's highway; For each wound I have a balm,—
Since I'm walking in the King's highway; Je-sus comes and walks with me;

Trust-ing still, I march along, Since I'm walking in the King's highway.
For I find the lions chained, Since I'm walking in the King's highway.
In the fight I wear a palm, Since I'm walking in the King's highway.
More in Him each day I see, Since I'm walking in the King's highway.

CHORUS.

Walking in the King's highway! I am walking in the King's highway! I am
highway!

happy in the Lord, I am trusting in His word, Since I'm walking in the King's highway.

No. 113. LEAD ME ALL THE WAY.

ADA BLENKHORN.　　　　　　　　　　　　Mrs. CARRIE B. ADAMS.

1. Lead me, Savior, gently lead, I pray, Lead me all a-long my pilgrim way;
2. Wilt Thou thro' life's journey be my Guide? Close beside me, blessed Lord abide;
3. Lead me, for the way I do not know; Lead me, for a - lone I can-not go;

Firmly hold me by Thy loving hand, Till I reach the promised, happy land.
Gent-ly whisper in my list'ning ear, Words of love my fainting heart to cheer.
Lead me,—Savior, Guide and Shepherd be, Lead, and I will gladly follow Thee.

CHORUS.

Sav-ior, lead .... me, gen-tly lead me; In Thy
Sav - ior, lead me, lead me, gen - tly lead me;

pleas - ant pastures feed me; Lead me, lead me ev'ry
In Thy pleas - ant pastures dai - ly feed me; Lead me, Sav - ior,

day, ... Kindly lead me all the way. .....
lead me ev-'ry day, Sav-ior, lead me, kind-ly lead me all a-long the way.

No. 114. WILL YOU DO WHAT YOU CAN?

C. H. G.

CHAS. H. GABRIEL.

1. Will you do what you can for the Mas-ter's cause, Will you
2. You have tast-ed the sweets of the Sav-ior's love, You have
3. Will you do what you can for the wan.-der-er, Who has

help to res-cue the lost in sin? Will you gird on the ar-
felt the glad-ness of sins for-giv'n; Will you do what you can
left the way that the Mas-ter trod? Will you scat-ter the rays

mor and go with pray'r That you may some soul from destruction win?
oth-er souls to win, Pointing them to joys that a-wait in heav'n?
of the light di-vine, That may lead the prod-i-gal back to God?

CHORUS. *Bass Solo.*

Yes, I'll glad-ly   gladly work for Je-sus, For He gave His
Yes, I'll glad - - ly work for Je - - sus, Who gave His

life, His life up-on the tree,   I will nev-er
life up-on the tree, ...   I will nev - - er grow a-

Will You Do What You Can?

I will nev-er wea-ry Till His smiling face, His smil-ing face I see.

-wea - - ry Un - til His smiling face I see. , . , ... ,

No. 115. BECAUSE HE LOVES US SO.

CHAS. E. NEAL.

1. We love to sing of Je - sus; He does so much we know,
2. We love to work for Je - sus, And ev - 'ry day to go
3. We love to pray to Je - sus, From whom all blessings flow;

To make us good and hap - py, Be-cause He loves us so.
And do some lit - tle kind - ness, Be-cause He loves us so.
And well we know He hears us, Be-cause He loves us so.

CHORUS.

We'll love Him, we'll love Him, While in this world be - low:

And then He'll take us home to heav'n, Because He loves us so.

No. 116. TRUST IN GOD.

W. P. BALFERN. H. N. LINCOLN.

1. Wheth-er with the few or ma-ny Ev-er work-ing for the Lord,
2. Do your best in joy or sor-row, Do your best by night or day,
3. Sun and stars and trees and flow-ers, Flowing streams and boundless sea,

Do your best and nev-er fal-ter, Ev-er lean-ing on His word.
Do your best in strength or weakness, Heed not what the world may say;
Ev - er work to cheer and help us,—Do their best, their serv-ice free;

Are you in the midst of con-flict, Full of troub-le and un-rest?
See the Mas-ter ev-er work-ing Ev-er at His best was He;
Do your best thro' Time's thick darkness, And the best your eyes shall see;

Sor-row will not last for-ev-er,—Trust in God and do your best.
Thro' His cries and tears and bleeding,—To the last He toiled for thee.
When the Lord and prince of work-ers Comes again, He'll welcome thee.

CHORUS.

Trust in God, and do your best, Trust in God . . . and do your
Trust in God and do your best, Trust in God and

Trust In God.

best, ... Do your best, and nev - er fal - ter, Ev - er
do your best,

leau-ing on is word, Trust in God . . . . . and do your best.
Trust in God

No. 117.   **WHO WILL GATHER?**

C. H. G.
CHAS. H. GABRIEL.

1. { Lo! the har - vest field is bend-ing, Who will reap the gold - en
{ There are ma - ny i - dly standing In the mar - ket and the

2. { See the ma - ny that are wait-ing, 'Round a - bout the gold - en
{ They have themes, they have sug-ges-tions, For the la - bor and the

3. { Has - ten, broth-er, to the har - vest, To the har - vest of the
{ So that when the Mas - ter call - eth, This shall be the wel-come

1
grain, Who will bear the sheaves a - way? }
field, All in i - dle - ness to - day; }
Lord! Gath-er sheaves from near and far, }

lane, But the (*Omit.*)
yield, But the (*Omit.*)
word:—"Blessed (*Omit.*)

2
} reap-ers, where are they?
} reap-ers, where are they?
} reap-ers; here they are!"

CHORUS.

Who will gath-er, who will gather? Who will gather in the golden grain?

COPYRIGHT, 1890, BY CHAS H. GABRIEL.

No. 118. COME, ALL YE PEOPLE.

COPYRIGHT, 1902, BY W. E. M. HACKLEMAN.

A. W. CONNER. CHAS. GOUNOD.

FULL CHORUS. *Maestoso.*

Come, all ye people, Come join with saints and an - gels; Sound forth the

prais-es Of Christ our Lord, once cru-ci-fied. Sing of His glo - ry, His gos-pel

preach in ev-'ry land Till all the nations shall crown Him King e - ter - nal.

Speak of His love, Of His love for all mankind; Tell how He loved, how He
O speak, O speak, He loved,

died, How He lives and reigns forever more. Praise we the Lord, Tho' a
He died, O praise, O praise,

Come, All Ye People.

host should encamp a - gainst us; In His love, by His pow'r He shall save us—His

name shall we praise for-ev - er.   Bless-ed   for - ev - er   Is the Lord of

our sal-va -·tion. Praise Him, men and angels, Sing His praise for-ev-er more. ·
ev-er-more.

Praise Him; Bow before His throne, Vic-tor over death, He dies no more. Reign, Thou

1   2

might-y Sav-ior, reigning now in glory, Reign ever more;   Reign for-ev-er more

* Use small notes if desirable.

No. 119. GRANDLY OUR HOST IS MARCHING.

JENNIE REE.

CHAS. H. GABRIEL.

1. Grand-ly   our host is   march-ing, And loud our   song of   joy - ous
2. Faith is   our dai - ly watch-word, Our hope, the prom-ise   of His

vic - to - ry   is   ring - ing!   Christ   is   our great com-
word that nev - er   fail - eth;   Trust - ing,   con - fid - ing,

man - der,   And   at His march-ing   or - ders   on   we   go   with
serv - ing,   In   ev - 'ry   time of   need His   love   and care   a -

sing - ing.   Ev - 'ry   land shall   our song re - ech - o,   And, by the
vail - eth.   Bless - ed   Mas - ter,   we hear Thee call - ing,   And with our

grace He gives us, ev - 'ry nation shall sing praise, Shall own our Lord, ac -
bat - tle cry of "Loy-al - ty" we march a-long; Come weal or woe, we'll

Grandly Our Host Is Marching.

cept His word, And un - to Him the voice of sup - pli - ca- tion raise.
on- ward go, Un - til in heav'n at last we sing the vic-tor's song.

CHORUS.

Onward we go with singing, Our message ringing, His kingdom nearer bringing;
On we go with sing-ing, sing-ing, On, His king-dom nearer bringing;

Out-ward the gates are swinging, That all the world may enter in; yes,
On, the gates are swing-ing, That the world may en - ter in; yes,

Onward, with pray'r and weeping, Our ranks are sweeping, Our faithful watches keep-ing;
On-ward go with pray'r and weep-ing, On-ward sweeping, watches keeping;

On, till the fruits of reap-ing Are garnered from the fields of sin.
On-ward, gath - er fruits of reap-ing from the fields of sin.

No. 120. WE SHALL BE SATISFIED.

F. M. D.

FRANK M. DAVIS.

1. Some day we shall be sat-is-fied, When in His
2. Some day we shall be sat-is-fied, When we shall
3. Some day we shall be sat-is-fied, When all our

1. Some day we shall be sat-is-fied, When in

like-ness we ap-pear; Shall know each oth-er as we're
meet Him face to face, And sing with angels round the
bur-dens are laid down, When we shall stand be-fore the

His likeness we ap-pear; Shall know each

known, When all that's dark shall be made clear.
throne, We're saved, we're saved from sin by grace.
King, And there receive the promised crown.

other as we're known, When all that's dark shall be made clear.

CHORUS.

Sat-is-fied, we shall be sat-is-fied, Some day we shall be sat-is-

fied; When in His likeness we appear, We shall be satisfied.

be sat-is-fied;

No. 121. NEARER THE CROSS.

FANNIE CROSBY.   Mrs. J. F. KNAPP.

1. "Near-er the cross!" my heart can say, I am coming near-er; Near-er the
2. Near-er the Christian's mer-cy seat, I am coming near-er; Feasting my
3. Near-er in pray'r my hope as-pires, I am coming near-er; Deep-er the

cross from day to day, I am com-ing near-er; Nearer the cross where
soul on man-na sweet, I am com-ing near-er; Stronger in faith, more
love my soul de-sires, I am com-ing near-er; Near-er the end of

Je - sus died, Near-er the fountain's crimson tide, Near-er my Sav-ior's
clear I see Je - sus who gave Himself for me; Near-er to Him I
toil and care, Near-er the joy I long to share, Near-er the crown I

wound-ed side, I am com-ing near-er, I am com-ing near-er.
still would be; I am com-ing near-er, I am com-ing near-er.
soon shall wear; I am com-ing near-er, I am com-ing near-er.

No. 122. PURITY.

Dr. E. H. STOKES.

CHAS. H. GABRIEL.

1. Thou art pure, O God, my Fa - ther, Like Thy-self, may I be pure;
2. Thou art pure, O, Ho - ly Sav - ior, White-robed, spotless, I would be;
3. Thou art pure, E - ter - nal Spir - it, Breathe Thy Spir-it in - to mine;
4. Fa - ther, Son, E - ter - nal Spir - it, Ev - er bless - ed Trin - i - ty,

Doubt-ing nev - er, but the rath - er, Make me of my cleans-ing sure.
Free from sin, O, bless - ed fa - vor, Make, O make me pure like Thee.
Let me now, from Thee, in-her - it Per - fect pu - ri - ty di - vine.
Faith o'er-comes my doubts' demer - it, I take Thee, O take Thou me.

CHORUS.

Make me pure, All - Per - fect Fa - ther, Thou art a - ble, cleanse me so:—
4th v. Praise, O praise, All - Per - fect Fa - ther, Thou hast cleansed me, this I know;

That I may be, hence, for - ev - er, Whi - ter than the Vir - gin Snow.
Keep, O keep me, hence, for - ev - er, Whi - ter than the Vir - gin Snow.

No. 123. GLORIA PATRI.

Glory be to the Father, and to the Son, And to the Ho-ly Ghost,
As it was in the beginning, is now, and ev - er shall be: World without end. A-men.

No. 124.   THE FIRM FOUNDATION.

1. How firm a foun-da-tion, ye saints of the Lord, Is laid for your
2. "Fear not, I am with thee, O be not dis-mayed, For I am thy
3. "When thro' the deep wa-ters I call thee to go, The riv-ers of
4. "When thro' fie-ry tri - als thy path-way shall lie, My grace all suf-

faith in His ex - cel-lent word! What more can He say, than to
God, I will still give thee aid; I'll strengthen thee, help thee, and
sor - row shall not o - ver-flow; For I will be with thee, thy
fi - cient, shall be thy sup-ply, The flame shall not hurt thee; I

you He hath said, To you, who for ref - uge to Je - sus have
cause thee to stand, Up - held by my gra-cious, om - ni - po - tent
tri - als to bless, And sanc - ti - fy to thee thy deep-est dis -
on - ly de - sign Thy dross to con-sume and thy gold to re-

fled? To you, who for ref - uge to Je - sus have fled?
hand, Up - held by my gra - cious, om - ni - po - tent hand.
tress, And sanc - ti - fy to thee thy deep - est dis - tress.
fine, Thy dross to con-sume and thy gold to re - fine.

5 "E'en down to old age all my people | 6 "The soul that on Jesus hath leaned
shall prove   [love,   for repose,
My sovereign, eternal, unchangeable | I will not, I will not desert to his foes;
And when hoary hairs shall their tem- | That soul, though all hell should en-
ples adorn,   [be borne.   deavor to shake,
Like lambs they shall still in my bosom | I'll never, no never, no never forsake!"

No. 125. MY JESUS, I LOVE THEE.

A. J. GORDON.

1. My Je - sus, I love Thee, I know Thou art mine; For Thee all the
2. I love Thee, be-cause Thou hast first lov - ed me, And purchased my
3. I'll love Thee in life, I will love Thee in death, And praise Thee as
4. In man-sions of glo - ry And end - less de-light, I'll ev - er a-

fol - lies Of sin I re-sign; My gra - cious Re - deem-er, My
par - don On Cal - va - ry's tree; I love Thee for wear-ing The
long as Thou lend - est me breath; And say when the death-dew Lies
dore Thee In heav - en so bright; I'll sing with the glit - ter - ing

Sav-ior art Thou, If ev - er I loved Thee, My Je - sus, 'tis now.
thorns on Thy brow; If ev - er I loved Thee, My Je - sus, 'tis now.
cold on my brow, If ev - er I loved Thee, My Je - sus, 'tis now.
Crown on my brow, If ev - er I loved Thee, My Je - sus, 'tis now.

No. 126. THOU THINKEST, LORD, OF ME.

E. D. MUND.   E. S. LORENZ.

1. A - mid the tri - als which I meet, A - mid the thorns that pierce my feet,
2. The cares of life come thronging fast, Up - on my soul their shadow cast;
3. Let shadows come, let shadows go, Let life be bright or dark with woe,

Thou Thinkest, Lord, of Me.

FINE.

One thought remains su-premely sweet, Thou thinkest, Lord, of me!
Their gloom reminds my heart at last, Thou thinkest, Lord, of me!
I am con-tent, for this I know, Thou thinkest, Lord, of me!

D. S.—*What need I fear since Thou art near, And think-est, Lord, of me.*

CHORUS.

D.S.

Thou thinkest, Lord, of me, (of me,) Thou thinkest, Lord, of me, (of me;)

No. 127. FROM GREENLAND'S ICY MOUNTAINS.

1. { From Greenland's i-cy mountains, From In-dia's cor-al strand; } Roll
   { Where Af-ric's sun-ny foun-tains, (*Omit*............. ....) }
2. { Shall we, whose souls are light-ed, With wis-dom free on high, } The
   { Shall we, to men be-night-ed, (*Omit*.......................) }
3. { Waft, waft, ye winds, His sto - ry, And you, ye wat-ers, roll, } It
   { Till, like a sea of glo - ry, (*Omit*...... ....) }

down their golden sand; From many an ancient riv - er, From many a palm-y
lamp of life de - ny? Sal - va-tion! oh, sal-va-tion! The joy-ful sound pro-
spreads from pole to pole; Till o'er our ran-somed na-ture, The Lamb for sinners

plain, They call us to de - liv - er, Their land from er-ror's chain.
claim, Till earth's re-mot-est na - tion Has learned Mes-si-ah's name.
slain, Re-deem-er, King, Cre - a - tor, In bliss re-turns to reign.

No. 128. MY JESUS, AS THOU WILT.

1. My Je - sus, as Thou wilt: O may Thy will be mine; In - to Thy
2. My Je - sus, as Thou wilt: Tho' seen thro' many-a tear, Let not my
3. My Je - sus, as Thou wilt: All shall be well for me; Each changing

hand of love I would my all re - sign. Thro' sor-row or thro' joy,
star of hope Grow dim or dis-ap - pear. Since Thou on earth hast wept
fu-ture scene I glad-ly trust with Thee. Straight to my home a - bove,

Conduct me as Thine own, And help me still to say, "My Lord, Thy will be done."
And sorrow'd oft alone, If I must weep with Thee, My Lord, Thy will be done.
I trav-el calm-ly on, And sing in life or death, "My Lord, Thy will be done."

No. 129. HOLY, HOLY, HOLY.

1. Ho-ly, ho-ly, ho-ly, Lord God Al-might-y! Ear-ly in the
2. Ho-ly, ho-ly, ho-ly! all the saints a-dore Thee, Casting down their
3. Ho-ly, ho-ly, ho-ly! tho' the darkness hide Thee, Tho' the eye of
4. Ho-ly, ho-ly, ho-ly, Lord God Al-might-y! All Thy works shall

Holy, Holy, Holy.

morn - ing our song shall rise to Thee; Ho - ly, ho - ly, ho - ly,
golden crowns around the glass-y sea; Cher- u - bim and seraphim
sin - ful man Thy glo - ry may not see; On - ly Thou art ho - ly!
praise Thy name, in earth, and sky, and sea; Ho - ly, ho - ly, ho - ly,

mer-ci - ful and might-y, God in three Persons, blessed Trin-i - ty!
fall-ing down before Thee, Which wert, and art, and evermore shalt be.
there is none be- side Thee, Per-fect in pow'r, in love, and pur - i - ty.
mer-ci - ful and might-y, God in three Persons, blessed Trin-i - ty!

No. 130.   ROCK OF AGES.

FINE.

1. Rock of A - ges, cleft for me, Let me hide my-self in Thee;

D. C.—*Be of sin the dou -ble cure,—Cleanse me from its guilt and pow'r.*

D. C.

Let the wa - ter and the blood, From Thy wounded side which flowed,

2 Not the labor of my hands
  Can fulfil the law's demands;
  Could my zeal no respite know,
  Could my tears forever flow,
  All for sin could not atone,—
  Thou must save, and Thou alone

3 Nothing in my hand I bring;
  Simply to Thy cross I cling;
  Naked, come to Thee for dress,

  Helpless, look to Thee for grace,—
  Vile, I to the Fountain fly,
  Wash me, Savior, or I die.

4 While I draw this fleeting breath,
  When my heart-strings break in death,
  When I soar to worlds unknown,
  See Thee on Thy judgment throne,
  Rock of Ages, cleft for me,
  Let me hide myself in Thee.

No. 131. MISSIONARY BATTLE HYMN.

WORDS COPYRIGHT, 1902, BY W. E. M. HACKLEMAN.

JESSIE BROWN POUNDS.   Tune: Battle Hymn of the Republic.

1. The earth shall know the glo-ry of the pres-ence of the Lord,
2. The lands that wait in dark-ness yet shall see the prom-ised day;
3. My soul, be hushed and pa-tient, God is now up - on His throne;

And the songs of ev - 'ry na - tion with the choirs of heav'n accord;
In the plac - es of the des - ert He shall make a ho - ly way;
O be pa - tient and be - liev-ing,—He is watch-ing o'er His own;

Then the hosts of sin and Sa - tan shall be vanquished at His word,
All the world shall know His coming and its kings shall own His sway,
He will claim the world for Je - sus, and His mighty pow'r make known,

CHORUS.

For God is march-ing on.   Glo - ry, glo-ry, hal-le - lu - jah!

Glo - ry, glo-ry, hal - le - lu - jah!   Our God is marching on.

No. 132   Jesus, my All.

1 Jesus, my all, to heaven is gone,
He whom I fix my hopes upon;
His track I see, and I'll pursue
The narrow way, till Him I view.
The way the holy prophets went,
The road that leads from banishment,
The Kings highway of holiness,
I'll go, for all His paths are peace.

2 This is the way I long have sought,
And mourned,because I found it not;
My grief a burden long has been,
Because I was not saved from sin.
The more I strove against its power,
I felt its weight and guilt the more;
'Till late I heard my Savior say
"Come hither, soul, I am the way."

3 Lo! glad I come; and Thou, blest lamb,
Shalt take me to Thee as I am;
Nothing but sin have I to give;
Nothing but love shall I receive.
Then will I tell to sinners 'round,
What a dear Savior I have found
I'll point to Thy redeeming blood.
And say, "Behold the way to God."

No. 133. Tell it to Jesus.

1 Are you weary, are you heavy-hearted
Tell it to Jesus, tell it to Jesus;
Are you grieving over joys departed?
Tell it to Jesus alone.

CHO.—Tell it to Jesus, tell it to Jesus,
He is a friend that's well known;
You have no other such a friend or brother,
Tell it to Jesus alone.

2 Do the tears flow down your cheeks
unbidden?
Tell it to Jesus, tell it to Jesus;[den?
Have you sins that to man's eye are hid.
Tell it to Jesus alone.

3 Do you fear the gathering clouds of
sorrow?
Tell it to Jesus, tell it to Jesus;[row?
Are you anxious what shall be tomor-
Tell it to Jesus alone.

4 Are you troubled at the tho't of dying?
Tell it to Jesus, tell it to Jesus;
For Christ's coming kingdom are you
sighing?
Tell it to Jesus alone.

No. 134   The Lily of the Valley.

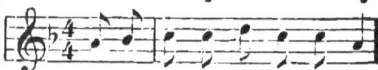

1 I have found a friend in Jesus, He's
every thing to me,
He's the fairest of ten thousand to
my soul;
The Lily of the Valley, in Him alone
I see,
All I need to cleanse and make me
fully whole;
In sorrow He's my comfort,in trouble
He's my stay,
He tells me every care on Him to roll,
He's the Lily of the Valley the bright
and Morning Star,
He's the fairest of ten thousand to my
soul.

CHO.—In sorrow He's my comfort, in
trouble He's my stay,
He tells me every care on Him to roll.
He's the Lily of the Valley,the bright
and Morning Star.
He's the fairest of ten thousand to my
soul.

2 He all my griefs has taken,and all my
sorrows borne;
In temptation He's my strong and
mighty tower;
I have all for Him forsaken, and all
idols torn
From my heart, and now He keeps
me by His power.
Though all the world forsake me and
Satan tempts me sore,   [goal.
Thro' Jesus I shall safely reach the
He's the Lily of the Valley,the bright
and Morning Star,
He's the fairest of ten thousand to my
soul.

3 He will never never leave me, nor yet
forsake me here.
While I live by faith and do His bless-
ed will;
A wall of fire about me, I've nothing
now to fear;
With His manna He my hungry soul
shall fill;
Then sweeping up to glory we see His
blessed face,
Where rivers of delight shall ever roll,
He's the Lily of the Valley,the bright
and Morning Star,
He's the fairest of ten thousand to my
soul.

No. 135.   I AM COMING.

W. G. FISCHER.

1. I am com - ing to the cross, I am poor, and weak and blind;
2. Here I give my all to Thee, Friends and time, and earthly store;
3. Je - sus comes! He fills my soul! Per - fect - ed in love I am;

CHO.—*I am trust-ing, Lord, in Thee, Dear Lamb of Cal - va - ry;*

I am count-ing all but dross, I shall full sal - va - tion find.
Soul and bod - y, thine to be,— Whol-ly Thine for - ev - er - more.
I am ev - 'ry whit made whole, Glo-ry, glo - ry to the Lamb.

Hum-bly at Thy cross I bow, Je - sus save me, save me now.

No. 136.   LORD, DISMISS US.

FINE.

1. Lord, dismiss us with Thy blessing, Fill our hearts with joy and peace;
2. Thanks we give and ad - o - ra - tion, For the gos - pel's joy-ful sound;
3. So, when-e'er the sig-nal's giv - en Us from earth to call a - way,

D. C. *O re - fresh us, O re - fresh us, Tráv'ling thro' this wil - der-ness.*
D. C. *May Thy presence, may Thy pres-ence With us ev - er - more be found.*
D. C. *May we ev - er, may we ev - er Reign with Christ in end - less day.*

D. C.

Let us each Thy love pos-sess-ing, Tri-umph in re-deem-ing grace.
May the fruits of Thy sal - va-tion In our hearts and lives a-bound.
Borne on an-gels' wings to heav-en, Glad the sum-mons to o - bey.

AVON.

No. 137.

1 Let Him to whom we now belong,
His Sovereign right assert;
And take up every thankful song
And every loving heart.

2 He justly claims us for His own,
Who bought us with a price;
The Christian lives to Christ alone;
To Christ alone he dies.

3 Jesus! Thine own at last receive;
Fulfil our heart's desire;
And let us to Thy glory live,
And in Thy cause expire.

4 Our souls and bodies we resign;
With joy we render Thee
Our all—no longer ours but Thine
To all eternity.

No. 138.

1 Alas! and did my Savior bleed?
And did my Sovereign die?
Would He devote that sacred head
For such a worm as I?

2 Was it for crimes that I have done,
He groaned upon the tree?
Amazing pity! grace unknown!
And love beyond degree!

3 Well might the sun in darkness hide,
And shut His glories in,   [died,
When Christ, the mighty Maker,
For man, the creature's sin.

4 Thus might I hide my blushing face,
While His dear cross appears;
Dissolve my heart in thankfulness,
And melt mine eyes to tears.

No. 139.

1 O for a closer walk with God,
A calm and heavenly flame;
A light to shine upon the road
That leads me to the Lamb!

2 Where is the blessedness I knew,
When first I saw the Lord?
When is the soul-refreshing view
Of Jesus and His word?

3 Return, O holy Dove, return.
Sweet messenger of rest! [mourn,
I hate the sins that make Thee
And drove Thee from my breast.

4 The dearest idol I have known,
Whate'er that idol be,
Help me to tear it from Thy throne,
And worship only Thee.

No. 140.

1 Come, Holy Spirit, heavenly Dove,
With all Thy quickening powers;
Kindle a flame of sacred love
In these cold hearts of ours.

2 Look how we grovel here below,
Fond of these earthly toys;
Our souls, how heavily they go,
To reach eternal joys.

3 Father, and shall we ever live
At this poor dying rate,
Our love so faint, so cold to Thee,
And Thine to us so great?

No. 141.

1 Come, humble sinner, in whose breast
A thousand thoughts revolve,
Come, with your guilt and fear oppressed,
And make this last resolve :—

2 I'll go to Jesus, though my sin
Like mountains round me close;
I know His courts, I'll enter in,
Whatever may oppose.

3 Prostrate I lie before His throne,
And there my guilt confess;
I'll tell Him, I'm a wretch undone
Without His sovereign grace.

No. 142. TAKE ME AS I AM.

CHARLOTTE ELLIOTT.

Melody by J. H. STOCKTON.
Har. by W. J. K.

1. Just as I am, without one plea, But that Thy blood was shed for me,
2. Just as I am, and wait-ing not To rid my soul of one dark blot—
3. Just as I am, tho' tossed a-bout, With many a conflict, many a doubt,
4. Just as I am, Thou wilt receive, Wilt welcome, pardon, cleanse, relieve,
5. Just as I am—Thy love unknown Has bro-ken ev-'ry bar-rier down;

And that Thou bidst me come to Thee, O Lamb of God, I come.
To Thee whose blood can cleanse each spot, O Lamb of God, I come.
With fears with-in, and woes with-out, O Lamb of God, I come.
Be-cause Thy prom-ise I be-lieve, O Lamb of God, I come.
Now to be Thine, yea, Thine a-lone, O Lamb of God, I come.

D. S.—since for sin Thy blood a-tones, O Lamb of God, I come.

REFRAIN.

Take me as I am, ... Take me as I am; . . . . . And
Take me, take me as I am, Take me, take me as I am;

No. 143.   SWEET HOUR OF PRAYER.

1. Sweet hour of prayer, sweet hour
   of prayer,
   That calls me from a world of care,
   And bids me at my Father's
   throne,
   Make all my wants and wishes
   known!
   In seasons of distress and grief
   My soul has often found relief,
   And oft escaped the tempter's
   snare,
   By thy return, sweet hour of
   prayer.

2. Sweet hour of prayer, sweet hour
   of prayer,
   Thy wings shall my petition bear,
   To Him whose truth and faithful-
   ness
   Engage the waiting soul to bless;
   And since He bids me seek His
   face,
   Believe His word, and trust His
   grace,
   I'll cast on Him my every care,
   And wait for thee, sweet hour of
   prayer.

—W. W. WALFORD.

SESSIONS.

L. O. EMERSON.

No. 144.

1 Lord, I am Thine, entirely Thine,
Purchased and saved by blood divine;
With full consent Thine I would be,
And own Thy sovereign right in me.

2 Grant one poor sinner more a place
Among the children of Thy grace;
A wreched sinner, lost to God,
But ransomed by Immanuel's blood.

3 Thine would I live,Thine would I die.
Be Thine through all eternity;
The vow is past beyond repeal,
And now I set the solemn seal.

4 Here, at that cross where flows the
blood
That bought my guilty soul for God,
Thee,my new Master, now I call.
And consecrate to Thee my all.

No. 145.

1 I thirst, Thou wounded Lamb of God,
To wash me in Thy cleansing blood;
To dwell within Thy wounds; then
pain
Is sweet, and life or death is gain.

2 Take my poor heart, and let it be
Forever closed to all but Thee :
Seal Thou my breast, and let me wear
That pledge of love forever there.

3 How blest are they who still abide
Close sheltered in Thy bleeding side !
Who thence their life and strength
derive,
And by Thee move, and in Thee live.

4 Hence our hearts melt, our eyes o'er-
flow,
Our words are lost. nor will we know
Nor will we think of aught beside;
"My Lord, my Love is crucified."

No. 146. OLD HUNDRED.—Doxology.

Praise God, from whom all blessings flow, Praise Him, all creatures here below;

Praise Him a-bove, ye heav'nly host; Praise Father, Son, and Ho-ly Ghost.

No. 147. GLORIOUS FOUNTAIN.

COWPER.

T. C. O'KANE.

1. { There is a fountain fill'd with blood, filled with blood, fill'd with blood,
   { And sinners plung'd beneath that flood, beneath that flood, beneath that flood,

2. { The dy-ing thief re-joiced to see, re-joiced to see, re-joiced to see,
   { And there may I, tho' vile as he, tho' vile as he, tho' vile as he,

There is a fountain filled with blood, Drawn from Immanuel's veins, }
And sin-ners plung'd beneath that flood, Lose all their guilt-y stains. }

The dy-ing thief re-joiced to see That fount-ain in his day, }
And there may I, tho' vile as he, Wash all my sins a-way. }

CHORUS.

Oh! glorious fountain! Here will I stay, And in Thee ever, Wash my sins a-way.

3 Thou dying Lamb, ||: thy precious blood, :||
Shall never lose its power,
Till all the ransom'd ||: Church of God, :||
Are saved, to sin no more.

4 E'er since by faith ||: I saw the stream, :||
Thy flowing wounds supply,
Redeeming love ||: has been my theme, :||
And shall be till I die.

No. 148. THE CLEANSING WAVE.

Mrs. PHŒBE PALMER.

Mrs. J. F. KNAPP.

1. { Oh, now I see the cleansing wave! The fount-ain deep and wide;
   { Jesus, my Lord, mighty to save,   Points to His wounded side.

The Cleansing Wave.

CHORUS.

{ The cleansing stream I see, I see! I plunge, and lo! it cleanseth me!
{ Oh, praise the Lord! it cleanseth me;   It cleanseth me—yes, cleanseth me.

2. I rise to walk in heaven's own light,
Above the world of sin, [white.]
With heart made pure and garments
And Christ enthroned within.

3 Amazing grace! 'tis heaven below
To feel the blood applied,
And Jesus, only Jesus know,
My Jesus crucified.

No. 149.   O HAPPY DAY.

1. { O hap-py day, that fix'd my choice On thee, my Sav-ior and my God!
   { Well may this glowing heart re-joice, And tell its rap-tures all a-broad.

2. { O hap-py bond, that seals my vows To Him that mer-its all my love!
   { Let cheerful an-thems fill His house, While to that sacred shrine I move.

3. { 'Tis done! the great transaction's done! I am my Lord's, and He is mine;
   { He drew me, and I followed on, Charm'd to confess the voice di-vine.

4. { Now rest, my long di-vid-ed heart; Fix'd on this blissful cen-tre, rest;
   { Nor ev-er from thy Lord de-part; With Him, of ev-'ry good possessed.

5. { High heav'n that heard the solemn vow, That vow renew'd shall daily hear,
   { Till in life's lat-est hour I bow, And bless in death a bond so dear.

FINE.

Hap-py day, hap-py day, When Je-sus washed my sins a-way!

D. S.

He taught me how to watch and pray, And live re-joic-ing ev-'ry day.

No. 150. I'M GLAD SALVATION'S FREE.

1. Come, ye that love the Lord, And let your joys be known;
2. Let those re - fuse to sing Who nev - er knew our God;
3. There we shall see His face, And - nev - er, nev - er sin;
4. Then let our songs a - bound. And ev - 'ry tear be dry;

CHO.—*I'm glad sal - va - tion's free, I'm glad sal - va - tion's free;*

Join in a song with sweet ac-cord, While ye surround the throne.
But chil - dren of the heav'nly King May speak their joys a - broad.
There, from the riv - ers of His grace, Drink end-less pleasures in.
We're marching thro' Immanuel's ground To fair - er worlds on high.

Sal - va - tion's free for you and me, I'm glad sal - va-tion's free.

No. 151. TAKE MY LIFE.

1. Take my life and let it be Con-se-crat-ed, Lord, to Thee; Take my hands and
2. Take my feet and let them be Swift and beautiful for Thee; Take my voice and
3. Take my lips and let them be Fill'd with messages from Thee; Take my silver
4. Take my moments and my days, Let them flow in endless praise; Take my in-tel-

let them move At the impulse of Thy love, At the impulse of Thy love.
let me sing, Always, on- ly for my King, Always, on - ly for my King.
and my gold, Not a mite would I withhold, Not a mite would I withhold.
lect and use Ev'ry pow'r as Thou shalt choose, Ev'ry pow'r as Thou shalt choose.

5 Take my will and make it Thine,
  It shall be no longer mine;
  Take my heart, it is Thine own,
  It shall be Thy royal throne.

6 Take my love, my God, I pour
  At Thy feet its treasured store;
  Take myself, and I will be
  Ever, only, all for Thee.

No. 152.   JESUS, LOVER OF MY SOUL.

FINE.

I. { Je - sus, lov - er of my soul, Let me to Thy bo - som fly,
   { While the nearer wa - ters roll, While the tempest still is high;

D. C.—*Safe in - to the ha - ven guide, Oh, re-ceive my soul at last.*

D. C.

Hide me, O my Sav-ior hide, Till the storm of life is past;

2 Other refuge have I none,
  Hangs my helpless soul on Thee;
Leave. oh. leave me not alone.
  Still support and comfort me.
All my trust on Thee is stayed,
  All my help from Thee I bring;
Cover my defenceless head
  With the shadow of Thy wing.

3 Thou, O Christ, art all I want.
  More than all in Thee I find;
Raise the fallen, cheer the faint,
  Heal the sick and lead the blind.
Just and holy is Thy name;
  I am all unrighteousness;
Vile and full of sin I am,
  Thou art full of truth and grace.

No. 153.   COME TO JESUS.

I. Come to Je - sus, Come to Je - sus, Come to Je - sus, just now;

Just now come to Je - sus, Come to Je - sus, just now.

2 He will save you.
3 He is able
4 Only trust Him.

5 Call upon Him.
6 He will hear you.
7 Look to Jesus.

8 He'll forgive you.
9 Don't reject Him.
10 Hallelujah, Amen.

No. 154. THERE IS A FOUNTAIN.

1. } There is a fountain fill'd with blood Drawn from Immanuel's veins, } Lose
And sinners plunged beneath that flood, (*Omit.*) Lose

D.C.—*And sinners plunged beneath that flood,* (*Omit.*) *Lose*

FINE.

all their guilty stains, Lose all their guilty stains, Lose all their guilty stains.
all their guilty stains.

D. C.

2 The dying thief rejoiced to see
That fountain in his day;
And there may I, tho' vile as he,
Wash all my sins away.

3 Dear dying Lamb, Thy precious blood
Shall never lose its power.
Till all the ransomed Church of God
Are saved, to sin no more.

4 E'er since by faith I saw the stream
Thy flowing wounds supply.
Redeeming love has been my theme,
And shall be till I die.

5 Then in a nobler, sweeter song,
I'll sing Thy power to save, [tongue
When this poor lisping stam'ring
Lies silent in the grave.

No. 155. LOVING KINDNESS.

1. A-wake, my soul, in joy-ful lays, And sing my great Redeemer's praise,

He just-ly claims a song from me, His lov-ing kind-ness, oh, how free!

Loving Kindness.

Lov-ing kindness, lov-ing kindness, His lov-ing kind-ness, oh, how free!

2 He saw me ruined by the fall,
Yet loved me notwithstanding all;
He saved me from my lost estate,
His loving kindness, oh, how great!
Loving kindness, loving kindness,
His loving kindness, oh, how great!

3 Tho' numerous hosts of mighty foes,
Tho' earth and hell my way oppose,
He safely leads my soul along,
His loving kindness, oh, how strong!
Loving kindness, loving kindness,
His loving kindness, oh, how strong!

No. 156.   AMERICA.

1. My coun - try, 'tis of thee, Sweet land of lib - er - t·
2. My na - tive coun - try, thee, Land of the no - ble f·
3. Let mu - sic swell the breeze, And ring from all the t.
4. Our Fa - thers' God, to Thee, Au - thor of lib - er -

Of thee I sing; Land where my fa - thers died, Land of the
Thy name I love; I love thy rocks and rills, Thy woods and
Sweet free-dom's song; Let mor - tal tongues a-wake, Let all that
To Thee we sing; Long may our 'land be bright, With freedom's

Cres.

Pil-grims' pride, From ev - 'ry mount-ain's side, Let free-dom ring.
tem-pled hills, My heart with rap ture thrills, Like that a - bove.
breathe par-take, Let rocks their si-lence break, The sound pro - long.
ho - ly light, Pro-tect us by Thy might, Great God, our King.

No. 157. NEARER, MY GOD, TO THEE.

1. Near-er, my God, to Thee, Near-er to Thee; E'en tho' it be a cross
2. Tho' like a wan-der-er, The sun gone down, Dark-ness be o-ver me,
3. There let the way ap-pear Steps un-to heav'n; All that Thou sendest me,
4. Then with my waking thot's Bright with Thy praise, Out of my stony griefs,
5. Or if, on joy-ful wing, Cleaving the sky; Sun, moon and stars forgot,

D. S.—*Near-er, my God, to Thee!*

FINE.   D. S.

That rais-eth me,   Still, all my song shall be—Nearer, my God, to Thee!
My rest a stone;   Yet in my dreams I'd be   Nearer, my God, to Thee!
n mer-cy given;   An-gels to beck-on me   Nearer, my God, to Thee!
th-el I'll raise;   So by my woes to be   Nearer, my God, to Thee!
p-ward I fly;   Still, all my song shall be.   Nearer, my God, to Thee!

ar-er to Thee!

158. ALL HAIL THE POWER.

1. All hail the pow'r of Je-sus' name, Let an-gels prostrate fall;

Bring forth the roy-al di-a-dem, And crown Him Lord of all.

All Hail the Power.

Bring forth the roy - al di - a - dem, And crown Him Lord of all.

2 Let every kindred, every tribe,
   On this terrestrial ball,
   ||:To Him all majesty ascribe,
   And crown Him Lord of all.:||

3 Oh, that with yonder sacred throng
   We at His feet may fall;
   ||:We'll join the everlasting song,
   And crown Him Lord of all.:||

No. 159. BRINGING IN THE SHEAVES.

1. { Sowing in the morning, sowing seeds of kindness, Sowing in the noontide
     { Waiting for the harvest, and the time of reaping, (*Omit.*)

and the dewy eves; We shall come rejoicing, bringing in the sheaves, Bringing in the

sheaves, bringing in the sheaves, We shall come rejoicing, bringing in the sheaves,

After repeat D. S. to Fine.

2 Sowing in the sunshine, sowing in the shadows,
   Fearing neither clouds nor winter's chilling breeze:
   By and by the harvest, and the labor ended,
   We shall come rejoicing, bringing in the sheaves.

3 Go then, ever weeping, sowing for the Master,
   Though the loss sustained our spirit often grieves;
   When our weeping's over, He will bid us welcome,
   We shall come rejoicing, bringing in the sheaves.

No. 160. WHERE HE LEADS ME.

1. I can hear the Sav - ior call-ing, I can hear the Sav - ior call-ing,
2. I'll go with Him thro' the gar-den, I'll go with Him thro' the gar-den,
3. I'll go with Him thro' the judgment, I'll go with Him thro' the judgment,
4. He will give me grace and glo - ry, He will give me grace and glo-ry,

CHO.—*Where He leads me I will fol - low, Where He leads me I will fol - low,*

Ad lib.

I can hear the Sav - ior call-ing, "Take thy cross, and follow, follow me."
I'll go with Him thro' the garden, I'll go with Him, with Him all the way.
I'll go with Him thro' the judg-ment, I'll go with Him, with Him all the way.
He will give me grace and glo-ry, And go with me, with Him all the way.

Where He leads me I will fol - low, I'll go with Him, with Him all the way.

No. 161. JESUS, I MY CROSS HAVE TAKEN.

1. Je - sus, I my cross have tak-en, All to leave and fol-low Thee;

FINE·

Na-ked, poor, despised, for-sak-en, Thou from hence my all shalt be;

D.S.—*Yet how rich is my con-di-tion, God and heav'n are still my own.*

Jesus, I My Cross Have Taken.

D.S.

Per-ish ev-'ry fond am-bi-tion,All I've sought,and hop'd,and known;

2 Let the world despise forsake me,
They have left my Savior too;
Human hearts and looks deceive me.
Thou art not, like man, untrue;
And, while Thou shalt smile upon me,
. God of wisdom, love and might,
Foes may hate, and friends may shun
Show Thy face and all is bright.[me,

3 Go, then, earthly fame and treasure!
Come, disaster, scorn and pain!
In Thy service, pain is pleasure;
With Thy favor, loss is gain :
I have called Thee, "Abba, Father,"
I have stayed my heart on Thee;[er,
Storms may howl,and clouds may gath-
· All must work for good to me.

No. 162.   REVIVE US AGAIN.

1. We praise Thee, O God! for the Son of Thy love,
2. We praise Thee, O God! for Thy Spir - it of light,
3. All glo - ry and praise to the Lamb that was slain,
4. All glo - ry and praise to the God of all grace,

For Je - sus who died and is now gone a - bove,
Who has shown us our Sav - ior and scat-tered our night,
Who has borne all our sins and has cleansed,ev -'ry stain,
·Who has bought us, and sought us, and guid - ed our ways,

REFRAIN.

Hal-le-lu-jah! Thine the glory;Hal-le-lu-jah! a-men! Re-vive us a-gain.

No. 163. THE GREAT PHYSICIAN.

FINE.

1. { The great Phy-si-cian now is near, The sym-pa-thiz-ing Je-sus, }
   { He speaks the drooping heart to cheer, Oh! hear the voice of Je-sus, }

2. { Your ma-ny sins are all for-giv'n, Oh! hear the voice of Je-sus, }
   { Go on your way in peace to heav'n And wear a crown with Je-sus, }

D. S.—*Sweet-est car-ol ev - er sung,* *Je - sus, bless - ed Je - sus.*

. REFRAIN.   D. S.

Sweet-est note in ser-aph song, Sweet-est name on mor-tal tongue;

3 All glory to the dying Lamb!
  I now believe in Jesus;
  I love the blessed Savior's name,
  I love the name of Jesus.

4 His name dispels my guilt and fear,
  No other name but Jesus;
  Oh! how my soul delights to hear
  The charming name of Jesus.

No. 164. HOW GENTLE GOD'S COMMAND.

1. How gen - tle God's commands! How kind His pre-cepts are!
2. Be - neath His watch-ful eye His   saints se - cure - ly dwell;
3. Why should this anx - ious load Press down your wea - ry mind?
4. His good - ness stands approved, Un - chang'd from day to day:

Come, cast your bur-dens on the Lord, And trust His con-stant care.
That hand which bears all na - ture up Shall guard His chil-dren well.
Haste to your heaven-ly Father's throne, And sweet re - fresh-ment find.
I'll drop my bur - den at His feet, And bear a song a - way.

No. 165. HOLY SPIRIT, FAITHFUL GUIDE.

D.C.

2 Ever present, truest Friend,
Ever near, Thine aid to lend,
Leave us not to doubt and fear,
Groping on in darkness drear.
When the storms are raging sore,
Hearts grow faint, and hopes give o'er,
Whisper softly, "Wanderer, come,
Follow me, I'll guide thee home."

1 Holy Spirit, faithful Guide,
Ever near the Christian's side,
Gently lead us by the hand,
Pilgrims in a desert land.
Weary souls, fore'er rejoice,
While they hear that sweetest voice
Whispering softly, "Wanderer, come,
Follow me, I'll guide thee home."

3 When our days of toil shall cease,
Waiting still for sweet release,
Nothing left but heaven and prayer,
Wondering if our names are there;
Wading deep the dismal flood,
Pleading naught but Jesus' blood;
Wisper softly, "Wanderer, come,
Follow me, I'll guide thee home."

No. 166.   WHAT A FRIEND.

1 What a friend we have in Jesus,
 All our sins and griefs to bear!
What a privilege to carry
 Everything to God in prayer!
Oh, what peace we often forfeit,
 Oh, what needless pain we bear,
All because we do not carry
 Everything to God in prayer!

2 Have we trials and temptations?
 Is there trouble anywhere?
We should never be discouraged,
 Take it to the Lord in prayer.

Can we find a friend so faithful,
 Who will all our sorrows share?
Jesus knows our every weakness,
 Take it to the Lord in prayer.

3 Are we weak and heavy laden,
 Cumbered with a load of care,
Precious Savior, still our refuge,
 Take it to the Lord in prayer.
Do thy friends despise, forsake thee?
 Take it to the Lord in prayer:
In His arms He'll take and shield thee,
 Thou wilt find a solace there.

No. 167. HOW CAN I BUT LOVE HIM?

J. E. RANKIN. BY PERMISSION. E. S. LORENZ.

1. So ten - der, so precious, My Sav-ior to me; So true and so
2. So pa-tient, so kind-ly Tow'rd all of my ways; I blun-der so
3. Of all friends the fairest And tru-est is He; His love is the
4. His beau ty, tho' bleeding And circled with thorns, Is then most ex-

REFRAIN.

gra - cious, I've found Him to be,
blind - ly— He love still re-pays.
rar - est That ev - er can be.
ceed - ing, For grief Him a-dorns.
} How can I but love Him? But

love Him, but love Him? There's no friend above Him, Poor sinner, for thee.

BOYLSTON.

No. 168.

1 A charge to keep I have;
  A God to glorify:
  A never-dying soul to save,
  And fit it for the sky.

2 To serve the present age,
  My calling to fulfill,
  O may it all my powers engage
  To do my Master's will.

3 Help me to watch and pray,
  And on Thyself rely;
  Assured if I my trust betray,
  I shall forever die.

No. 169.

1 And can I yet delay
  My little all to give?
  To tear my soul from earth away,
  For Jesus to receive?

2 Nay, but I yield, I yield!
  I can hold out no more;
  I sink by dying love compell'd,
  And own the Conqueror!

3 Come, and possess me whole,
  Nor hence again remove;
  Settle and fix my wavering soul
  With all Thy weight of love.

No. 170. MUST JESUS BEAR THE CROSS.

1. Must Je-sus bear the cross a - lone,And all the world go free?
2. The con -se-cra-ted cross I'll bear Till death shall set me free;
3. Up - on the crys-tal pavement,down At Je - sus' pier-ced feet,
4. Oh, precious cross!oh,glorious crown!Oh res-ur-rec-tion day!

No, there's a cross for ev-'ry one, And there's a cross for me.
And then go home my crown to wear, For there's a crown for me.
With joy I'll cast my gold-en crown,And His dear name re-peat.
Ye an-gels from the stars come down And bear my soul a - way.

No. 171.
I Love to Tell the Story.
Key of A♭.

1 I love to tell the story
Of unseen things above,
Of Jesus and His glory,
Of Jesus and His love.
I love to tell the story,
Because I know 'tis true;
It satisfies my longings
As nothing else can do.

CHO.—I love to tell the story,
'Twill be my theme in glory,
To tell the old, old story
Of Jesus and His love.

2 I love to tell the story:
More wonderful it seems
Than all the golden fancies
Of all our golden dreams.
I love to tell the story,
It did so much for me;
And that is just the reason,
I tell it now to thee.

3 I love to tell the story,
For those who know it best
Seem hungering and thirsting
To hear it like the rest.
And when, in scenes of glory,
I sing the new, new song,
'Twill be the old, old story
That I have loved so long.

CATERINE HANKEY.

No. 172.
Marching to Zion.
Key of G.

1 Come, ye that love the Lord,
And let your joys be known,
Join in a song with sweet accord,
Join in a song with sweet accord,
And thus surround the throne,
And thus surround the throne.

CHO.—We're marching to Zion,
Beautiful, beautiful Zion,
We're marching upward to Zion,
The beautiful city of God.

2 Let those refuse to sing
Who never knew our God;
But children of the heav'nly King,
But children of the heav'nly King,
May speak their joys abroad.
May speak their joys abroad.

3 The hill of Zion yields,
A thousand sacred sweets,
Before we reach the heav'nly fields,
Before we reach the heav'nly fields,
Or walk the golden streets,
Or walk the golden streets.

4 Then let our songs abound,
And every tear be dry, [ground,
We're marching through Immanuel's
We're marching through Immanuel's
To fairer worlds on high, [ground,
To fairer worlds on high.

ISAAC WATTS.

No. 173.   O DAY OF REST AND GLADNESS.

1. { O   day   of   rest and glad-ness,   O   day   of   joy and light,   }
   { O   balm   of   care and sad-ness, Most beau-ti-ful most bright: }
2. { On thee,   at   the   cre-a-tion, The light first had its birth;   }
   { On thee,   for   our   sal-va-tion, Christ rose from depths of earth,   }

On thee, the high and low-ly, Through a - ges joined in   tune,
On thee, our Lord, vic - to - rious, The Spir - it   sent from heav'n;

Sing "Ho - ly,   ho - ly,   ho - ly,"   To   the great God Tri-une.
And thus on   thee, most glo - rious,   A   tri - ple light was giv'n.

3 To-day on weary nations
  The heavenly manna falls,
To holy convocations
  The silver trumpet calls,
Where gospel light is glowing
  With pure and radiant beams,
And living water flowing
  With soul-refreshing streams.

4 New graces ever gaining
  From this our day of rest,
We reach the rest remaining
  To spirits of the blest;
To Holy Ghost be praises,
  To Father, and to Son;
The Church her voice upraises
  To Thee, blest Three in One.

No. 174.   JESUS IS MINE!

1. Fade, fade, each earth-ly joy, Je - sus   is   mine! Break, ev - 'ry
2. Tempt not   my soul   a - way, Je - sus   is   mine! Here would I
3. Fare - well,   ye dreams of night, Je - sus   is   mine! Lost   in   this
4. Fare - well, mor - tal - i - ty, Je - sus   is   mine! Wel-come, e -

Jesus Is Mine.

ten-der tie, Je - sus is mine! Dark is the wil - der-ness,
ev - er stay, Je - sus is mine! Per-ish-ing things of clay,
dawning light, Je - sus is mine! All that my soul has tried
ter - ni - ty, Je - sus is mine! Wel-come,oh,loved and blest,

Earth has no rest-ing place, Je-sus a-lone can bless, Je - sus is mine!
Born but for one brief day, Pass from my heart a-way, Je - sus is mine!
Left but a dis-mal void, Je-sus has sat - is - fied, Je - sus is mine!
Wel-come,sweet scenes of rest, Welcome, my Savior's breast, Je - sus is mine!

No. 175. I STRETCH MY HANDS TO THEE.

CHARLES WESLEY.   Tune: I DO BELIEVE. C. M.

1. Fa - ther, I stretch my hands to Thee, No oth - er help I know;
2. What did Thine on - ly Son en - dure, Be-fore I drew my breath;
CHO.— I do be-lieve, I now be-lieve, That Je - sus died for me,

If Thou with-draw Thyself from me, Ah, whither shall I go?
What pain,what la - bor to se - cure, My soul from end-less death!
And thro' His blood, His precious blood, I shall from sin be free.

3 O Jesus, could I this believe,
   I now should feel Thy power;
   And all my wants Thou wouldst re-
   In this accepted hour.   [lieve,

4 Author of faith, to Thee I lift
   My weary, longing eyes;
   O let me now receive that gift!
   My soul without it dies.

No. 176. SAVIOR, PILOT ME.

FINE.

1. Je-sus, Sav-ior, pi-lot me O-ver life's tem-pest-uous sea;

Chart and com-pass came from Thee: Je-sus, Sav-ior, pi-lot me.

D.C.

Unknown waves be-fore me roll, Hid-ing rock and treacherous shoal;

2 When the apostle's fragile bark
   Struggled with the billow's dark.
On the stormy Galilee,
Thou didst walk upon the sea;
And when they beheld Thy form,
Safe they glided through the storm.

3 As a mother stills her child,
   Thou canst hush the ocean wild;
Boisterous waves obey Thy will

When Thou sayest to them,"Be still!"
Wondrous Sovereign of the sea,
Jesus, Savior, pilot me.

4 When at last I near the shore,
   And the fearful breakers roar
'Twixt me and the peaceful rest,
Then, while leaning on Thy breast,
May I hear Thee say to me,
"Fear not, I will pilot thee!"

No. 177. I Gave My Life.

1 I gave my life for thee,
   My precious blood I shed,
That thou might'st ransomed be,
   And quickened from the dead.
‖: I gave, I gave my life for thee, :‖
What hast thou given for me?

2 My Father's house of light,
   My glory-circled throne
I left, for earthly night,
   For wand'rings sad and lone.
‖: I left, I left it all for thee, :‖
Hast thou left aught for me?

3 I suffered much for thee,
   More than my tongue can tell,
Of bitterest agony.
   To rescue thee from hell;
‖: I've borne, I've borne it all for thee, :‖
What hast thou borne for me?

4 And I have brought to thee,
   Down from my home above,
Salvation full and free,
   My pardon and my love;
‖: I bring, I bring rich gifts to thee, :‖
What hast thou brought to me?

         F. R. HAVERGAL.

No. 178.
Take The Name Of Jesus.

Key, A♭

1 Take the name of Jesus with you,
   Child of sorrow and of woe;
It will joy and comfort give you,
   Take it, then, where'er you go.

CHO.—Precious name, O how sweet,
   Hope of earth and joy of heaven;
Precious name, O how sweet,
   Hope of earth and joy of heaven.

2 Take the name of Jesus ever,
   As a shield from every snare;
If temptations round you gather,
   Breathe that holy name in prayer.

3 Oh! the precious name of Jesus;
   How it thrills our souls with joy,
When His loving arms receive us,
   And His songs our tongues employ.

4 At the name of Jesus bowing,
   Falling prostrate at His feet,
King of kings in heav'n we'll crown Him,
   When our journey is complete.

        Mrs. LYDIA BAXTER.

No. 179. COME, LET US JOIN.

1. Come, let us join our cheerful songs With angels round the throne;
2. "Wor-thy the Lamb that died,"they cry,"To be ex- alt - ed thus!"
3. Je - sus is wor - thy to receive Hon - or- and pow'r di-vine;
4. Let all that dwell a -bove the sky, And air,and earth,and seas,
5. The whole cre-a - tion join in one, To bless the sa - cred name

Ten thousand thousand are their tongues,But all their joys are one.
"Wor-thy the Lamb!" our lips re - ply, "For He was slain for us."
And blessings,more than we can give, Be,Lord,for -ev - er Thine!
Con-spire to lift Thy glo-ries high.And speak Thine end- less praise.
Of Him who sits up -on the throne And to a-dore the Lamb!

No. 180. HARK! TEN THOUSAND.

FINE.

1. { Hark! ten-thousand harps and voices,Sound the note of praise a-bove; }
   { Je-sus reigns,and heav'n re-joic - es, Je - sus reigns, the God of love, }
2. { Je-sus, hail!whose glo ry brightens,All a-bove,and gives it worth; }
   { Lord of life, Thy smile enlightens,Cheers and charms Thy saints on earth. }

D.C.—*Hal- le - lu - jah, Hal - le - lu-jah! Hal - le - lu - jah, A - men.*

D.C.

See, He sits on yonder throne; Je-sus rules the world a - lone;
See, He sits on yon-der throne,Je-sus rules the world a - lone;
When we think of love like Thine, Lord,we own it love di- vine;
When we think of love like Thine, Lord we own it love di- vine;

3 King of glory reign forever;
Thine an everlasting crown;
Nothing from Thy love shall sever
Those whom Thou hast made Thine own;
Happy objects of Thy grace,
Destined to behold Thy face.

4 Savior, hasten Thine appearing;
Bring, oh, bring the glorious day,
When, the awful summons hearing,
Heaven and earth shall pass away;
Then with golden harps we'll sing,
"Glory, glory to our King."

No. 181. COME, SINNER, COME.

W. E. WITTER.   H. R. PALMER.

1. { While Je-sus whis-pers to   you,Come,sinner, come!
    { While we are pray-ing for   you,Come,   sin-ner, come!
2. { Are   you too heav - y   la - den?Come,sinner, come!
    { Je - sus will bear your bur - den,Come,   sin-ner, come!
3. { Oh,   hear His tend - er plead-ing,Come,sinner, come!
    { Come,and re-ceive the bless-ing,Come,   sin-ner, come!

{ Now is the   time to own Him,Come,sin-ner,come!
{ Now is the   time to know Him,Come,   sin-ner,come!
{ Je - sus will   not de-ceive you;Come,sinner, come!
{ Je - sus can   now re-deem you;Come,   sin-ner.come!
{ While Je-sus whis-pers to   you, Come,sinner,come!
{ While we are pray-ing for   you, Come.   sin-ner,come!

No. 182. COME, YE SINNERS.

FINE.

1. Come, ye' sin-ners, poor and need-y,Weak and wounded,sick and sore; }
   Je - sus read-y stands to   save you Full of   pit - y, love and pow'r. }

D.C.—*Glo-ry, hon-or, and   sal - va - tion,Christ the Lord,has come to reign.*

CHORUS.   D.C.

Turn to the Lord, and seek sal-va-tion.Sound the praise of His dear name.

2 Now, ye needy, come and welcome,
   God's free bounty glorify;
   True belief and true repentance,
     Every grace that brings you nigh.
3 Let not conscience make you linger,
   Nor of fitness fondly dream;

All the fitness He requireth,
   Is to feel your need of Him.
4 Come, ye weary, heavy laden,
   Bruised and mangled by the fall,
   If you tarry till you're better,
     You will never come at all.

No. 183. GOD BE WITH YOU,

J. E. RANKIN, D. D.   W. G. TOMER.

1. God be with you till we meet a-gain,   By   His councels guide,up-
2. God be with you till we meet a-gain,'Neath His wings se - cure - ly
3. God be with you till we meet a-gain,When life's per - ils thick con-
4. God be with you till we meet a-gain, Keep love's ban-ner float-ing

hold   you,   With His sheep se - cure - ly fold   you,
hide   you,   Dai - ly man - na still di - vide you,
found you,   Put His arms un - fail - ing round you,
o'er   you,   Smite death's threat'ning wave be - fore - you,

CHORUS.

God be with you till we meet a-gain. Till we meet, ... till we
Till we meet, till we
meet,   Till we meet at Je - sus' feet   Till we
meet, till we meet,   Till we meet,

meet,   till we meet,   God be with you till we meet again.
Till we meet,Till we meet,till we meet,

INDEX.

TITLES—Roman.   FIRST LINES—*Italic.*

INDEX—Continued.

159

INDEX—Continued.

160

www.ingramcontent.com/pod-product-compliance
Lightning Source LLC
Chambersburg PA
CBHW020554270326

41927CB00006B/842